THE LIVES OF SALMON

THE LIVES OF SALMON
An Illustrated Account of the Life-history
of the Atlantic Salmon

Alan Youngson and David Hay

SWAN·HILL
PRESS

First published in the UK in 1996
by Swan Hill Press, an imprint of Airlife Publishing Ltd

British Library Cataloguing in Publication Data
 A catalogue record for this book is available from the British Library

ISBN 1 85310 597 X

Typeset by Litho Link Ltd, Welshpool, Powys, Wales.
Printed in Singapore by Kyodo Printing Co (S'pore) Pte Ltd.

Swan Hill Press
an imprint of Airlife Publishing Ltd
101 Longden Road, Shrewsbury SY3 9EB

Contents

Preface

Scientists are often taken to task for failing to bring their findings and ideas to the notice of the widest possible audience. This volume is our attempt to avoid this charge – or at least to avoid it being repeated. Our theme deals with a conceptually difficult area, touching as it does on genetics, but we have endeavoured to present the facts and the arguments in a straightforward manner. It is our hope that this book will be enjoyed and understood by all those with an interest in salmon, irrespective of their background.

One of the most intriguing aspects of the study of salmon is that the details of their lives differ everywhere they occur. However, it is necessary to start somewhere, and this account is centred on the work of the group within the Freshwater Fisheries Laboratory to which we belong, although it draws freely on published research from other sources. We would like to acknowledge the contributions made by our colleagues and associates Bob Buck, Mike Donaghy, Andy Ferguson, Neil Fraser, Tony Hawkins, Bill Jordan, David Knox, John Mackenzie, Iain McLaren, Anne McLay, Sandy Mitchell, Dick Shelton, Peter Smith, John Taggart, Diogo Tomaz, Eric Verspoor and John Webb.

Salmon leaping at Buchanty Spout on the River Almond. The most prominent fish is a female, judging by her shape and colouration. Salmon are capable of passing the Falls of Orrin at Fairburn on the River Conon in Ross-shire which exceed 3.5m in height. In his book *Ecology and Management of Atlantic Salmon*, Derek Mills presents a photograph of a salmon making this leap.

Introduction

The Atlantic salmon is one of a group of species that lead their lives in the rivers and the oceans of the northern hemisphere. All the species inhabit fresh water at some stage in their lives; some are restricted to fresh water but most split their lives between fresh water and the sea. As adults, fish of the latter type feed in sea water but return to fresh water to spawn. The coho, chum, pink, sock-eye and chinook salmons of the Pacific Ocean and the Atlantic salmon of Europe and eastern North America all behave in this way. The lives of all the species are similar in some respects but in others they differ substantially, and each species is unique. All the species are of great interest from the commercial, sporting and scientific points of view.

The various species differ in the extent to which they rely on fresh water. They all use fresh water as a temporary habitat for their progeny but Atlantic salmon are among those that rely on streams and rivers to the greatest extent of all. Young Atlantic salmon remain in fresh water for at least one year, but more often for several years, before they leave for the sea to begin the adult phase of their lives. Even as adults they make great use of fresh water, not just for spawning, but for refuge too. Some Atlantic salmon return to fresh water and remain there for as long as a year before they spawn.

Atlantic salmon occur in clean, cool rivers on both the eastern and western Atlantic coasts. In Europe, they range from the rivers of Arctic Russia and Iceland, through Norway, Sweden, Finland, the United Kingdom, Ireland and France, as far as northern Spain. In North America, they spawn freely in the rivers of Labrador, Quebec, Newfoundland, Nova Scotia, New Brunswick and Maine. Over the past century, however, gaps have been opened in this range for a variety of reasons that are all attributable – directly or indirectly – to man's activities. For example, salmon are rare now in some major rivers, such as the Thames, the Rhine and the New England rivers, which once supported notable fisheries but can no longer do so.

Although most Atlantic salmon feed in the sea at some stage in their lives, there are exceptions to this general rule. In most streams, some small males become sexually mature without ever leaving fresh water. Only rarely do females become mature at this stage. In some locations, however, none of the salmon ever leave fresh water. These are the so-called land-locked Atlantic salmon. Land-locked salmon of both sexes live and breed without migrating to the sea. Despite their name, they do not occur only in places that are without access to the sea. Indeed, in some locations, land-locked salmon and sea-going salmon lead their lives in close proximity, but separately and without interbreeding. Land-locked salmon are rare in Europe, although isolated populations are known to exist in Norway, Sweden and Russia. They are also present in the lakes of eastern America and quite common in Newfoundland, where many separate populations exist.

In general, however, the salmon is an international fish, ranging freely among the jurisdictions of different nations at different times and through international waters. As a result, they fall within the care of different parties at different stages in their lives. Crucially, however, they return as adults to the rivers and streams from which they came – a recurring theme in this account – and this dictates how responsibility for the continued wellbeing of salmon stocks and the continued productivity of the fisheries must be apportioned. Ultimately, river managers bear responsibility for ensuring that each river's stock remains abundant, vigorous and varied. In return, the privilege of making the final harvest belongs to the same river's anglers. It is because salmon home that local management can be practised in the knowledge that some of the benefits will go to those who must bear all the costs.

Tagging a small grilse kelt moving down the Gander River in Newfoundland in early summer, on its way back towards the sea. The Gander is among Newfoundland's larger rivers. Temporary fences (more than 100m long) are put in place after the spring floods have passed. The fences span the river's width, deflecting kelts moving downstream into the trap shown in the photograph. In spite of their fine appearance, few Gander kelts are recaptured in later years. As a general rule, this is the fact of kelts everywhere – even well-mended kelts usually fail to survive their second spell at sea.

Fishing the Dee with companion and ghillie. There is no agreed method for assessing the economic worth of salmon angling. But, by all estimates, local communities and river proprietors benefit substantially from visiting anglers wherever salmon run the rivers.

It has been known for a very long time that salmon home. The phenomenon was discovered by marking young fish in such a manner that they could be recognised later. In the seventeenth century, Walton, in *The Compleat Angler*, described tying 'a riband, or some known tape or thread, in the tail of some young Salmons . . . as they swimmed towards the salt water'. Interestingly, Walton also described their recapture 'with the known mark at the same place, at their return from the sea, which is usually about six months after'. He was mistaken in this latter respect: the shortest delay before migrant salmon return to fresh water is now known to be about 12 months. But he was correct, in noting that the fish were recaptured near where they had been marked.

Interestingly, the mistake that Walton made was repeated 200 years later, in interpreting recaptures of fish marked as smolts at Stormontfield on the River Tay. In 1907, Calderwood described how these studies also gave rise to the belief that grilse returned to fresh water in the year of their going to sea. He gave greater credence to conflicting evidence obtained in other experiments carried out by the Tweed Commissioner at about the same time. Indeed, the matter was resolved shortly before Calderwood published, when the results became known of the tagging of 6500 salmon smolts with silver wires, at Kinfauns on the River Tay in 1905. As Calderwood had anticipated, the first recaptures of marked adults were made in 1906, more than a year later, and all the recaptures were made in the vicinity of the Tay.

Homing has profound consequences for salmon fisheries management and for the biology of the salmon themselves. Through homing, salmon have come to belong to separate breeding units or populations that can be regarded as independent of one another to a considerable extent.

The decaying carcase of a large male salmon with a well-developed kype. The kype is an overdevelopment of the cartilages of the extremities of the upper and lower jaws. Development occurs towards full sexual maturity under the influence of high levels of the male hormones and is especially pronounced in large males. In extreme cases, the developing lower jaw may protrude through the upper one. Presumably, the kype is a sexual characteristic that proves intimidatory to competing males or attractive to females. Many males die in autumn after spawning. This carcase has been hauled from the water and abandoned by a predator. Later, it was frozen and dehydrated in the winter snow. The carcasses of kelts provide sustenance throughout the winter for a number of scavenging species, including some birds and mammals. Ultimately, all the nutrients a kelt's carcase contains will be recycled near to the stream where it dies.

The Kinfauns studies were among the first truly scientific investigations of the behaviour of salmon. They were conducted in a systematic and methodical way on large numbers of fish. Since then, the Atlantic salmon has been much studied, and a considerable amount is now known about its life and habits. For scientists, the species has been of particular interest partly because of its commercial value, partly because it is relatively accessible while in fresh water and partly because of its complex life cycle and varied lifestyle. Although some anglers share the scientists' interest all these matters, none of them fully explains the anglers' regard for the species. For them (and for many scientists, too), the salmon appears to have a special significance that most other species of fish cannot match and none exceed.

In the following chapters we will examine the lives of salmon closely. We will construct a framework within which salmon fisheries and their management may be considered. In fact, as we shall see, the fisheries themselves ought really to be a secondary concern. Sound salmon fisheries are based on vigorous and diverse populations, and we will attempt to show that it is these that should first be targeted for management. Our framework will be of interest to the reflective angler and of value, perhaps, to the inventive one. It must be recognised however, that the salmon's life is not yet fully understood. Indeed, it has been necessary to shade in some of the gaps in present knowledge to create the framework we will present. Future research work will almost certainly require that our framework be modified – but perhaps not in the most crucial respects.

Anglers and scientists use different criteria in deciding which aspects of their knowledge of salmon are interesting or true. Like most other creatures, salmon are very variable in all aspects of their lives, and scientists acknowledge this. Indeed, accepting that it is impossible to describe all the variation that exists, scientists

A midsummer's day fish of 12lb (5.4kg) on a bed of thyme.

resort to the concept of probability. They attempt to describe the greater part of the variation that exists and hold that what happens most of the time is likely to be 'true'. Of course, to achieve this, they discard some of the information they collect – the small part of it that is most at odds with the rest. Although scientists (like everyone else) may find them interesting, freak occurrences and bizarre exceptions form no part of the scientific account. In comparing scientists' accounts with his own experience, the angler must bear this in mind.

Angling for salmon is a somewhat contrived sport. Anglers endeavour to capture fish within the self-imposed constraints of etiquette and using inefficient fishing methods and equipment that, even today, remains rudimentary in design. In general, these constraints are designed to make the sport difficult and, particularly, to maximise the salmon's role in its own capture. In essence, angling is about developing and deploying tactics under adverse conditions in the hope of succeeding against the odds. The proficient angler develops personal strategems for different beats, different lies, different times of year and different conditions, and derives the greatest satisfaction from each occasional success. For most anglers, tactics are based on an informal understanding of the lives of salmon, gleaned from personal experience or from conversation with companions. We believe that this sort of knowledge can be enriched by an understanding of the formal biology of salmon, to the greater enjoyment of the pastime and as a source of interest in itself.

CHAPTER 1

Life in Streams and Rivers

Towards the end of the year, salmon that have returned from the sea in previous months leave their lies and complete the last part of their journey home. By now they show full spawning colours. Males take on a mottled orange-red and females a dark grey appearance towards spawning time, in sharp contrast to the silvery coloration of both sexes when they enter rivers. Spawning is the culmination of life for both pairing fish and life begins for the next generation as eggs are shed by females into gravel nests and fertilised by males. Some of the spent fish, now known as kelts, will survive to regain condition and return in later years to spawn again. For many adults however, the first spawning is also the last; death often follows quickly as a result of weakness and disease.

A well-mended kelt caught in February. Fish like these can be mistaken for fresh springers by the unwary angler.

Spent females often move away from the spawning areas fairly quickly, but males tend to remain there longer, patrolling or lying in secure places nearby. For some kelts the journey back to the sea must be quite rapid since in former years, when the ocean fisheries north of the Faroe Islands were still being pursued, kelts were caught there in late winter. Others make slower progress back towards the sea. Indeed, some are caught in rivers in the early months of the salmon fishing season, taking anglers' lures intended for fresh spring fish. Most kelts are easily recognised by their still poor condition. Thinness of body, a distended vent, frayed fins and skin abrasions infected with pale, woolly fungal growth mark them down quite clearly. But other kelts are still vigorous, healthy fish and are often difficult to distinguish from maiden spring salmon. Indeed, some well-mended kelts pay the price for their bright condition at the hands of optimistic or inexperienced anglers. To the tutored eye, however, a slight thinness and the unusual intensity of their renewed silvering gives even well-mended kelts away. All the kelts that have survived spawning leave fresh water again for the sea, long before their progeny emerge from the gravel nests (or redds) in which the eggs have lain all winter.

Salmon eggs are about 5mm in diameter, although egg size varies and smaller females tend to produce slightly smaller eggs. By the standards of most other fishes, salmon embryos develop for a long time before hatching and the young fish are unusually large when they first become self-reliant. Each egg contains all the nutrients needed to sustain the development that goes on unseen within the redd. So salmon eggs are large compared with those of most other fish species.

The initial union of sperm and egg forms the first single cell of the new embryo. This cell divides into two, and these new cells divide in their turn to form four and so on, until the embryo comprises countless numbers of cells. All the time, these cells are being organised into body structures until, in late winter, the embryo becomes recognisably fish-like within the egg. Its dark eyes in particular, become noticeable through the translucent membrane of the shell.

At some point in late spring the young fish, or alevins, already about 20mm long, will break free of the egg membrane. After hatch they remain within the gravel of the redd for several more weeks. During this time, they continue to be sustained by the original resources of the egg and the yolk-sac remains prominently attached to the belly surface of the young fish. As the reserves of yolk become exhausted, the alevins finally make their way upwards through the gravel of the redd, emerging to begin life in the stream itself. Independent now, each alevin becomes engaged in a fierce competition for supremacy and for life itself. This struggle will last for the rest of the fish's life, but it starts with a particularly brutal intensity.

Juvenile salmon are solitary animals and each needs enough space on the stream bed to give it the shelter and the food it requires. The number of eggs laid often exceeds the capacity of the stream to provide territories for all the emerging fish, and the area of stream bed that is available thus limits their total number. Rather than reducing the size of individual territories to accommodate the others, the fittest individuals seize what they require. The weaker fish perish, deprived of the

Salmon eggs in April, shortly before hatching time, sampled from a redd made in November. The eggs are about 5mm in diameter and they are lying on a sampling net among small pieces of spawning gravel. A single dead egg, opaque and white, can be seen centrally. It has been dead for some time. Indeed, the eggs may never have been fertile. In the end, eggs that are not viable are broken down by fungi and bacteria.

The embryos within these living eggs are developed sufficiently to be recognisable through the translucent eggshell. The dark spots seen in some of the eggs are the embryo's developing eyes and in some eggs both eyes can be seen.

A newly hatched salmon alevin. The eggshell has been discarded. The young fish is recognisably fish-like although it remains poorly developed. The skin is not yet pigmented. As a result, the developing muscle blocks can be seen through it as barred structures running at right angles to the body's length. The remnant of the yolk-sac that contained the nutrients that supported the embryo during its development remains attached to the underside of the body. The yolk-sac will continue to provide nourishment for a further four to six weeks while the young fish remains within the redd. Fat globules can be seen within the yolk. The sac has a prominent blood vessel that carries nutrients to the alevin's body. When the yolk-sac becomes completely absorbed the young fish must become self-reliant.

resources they need for life. Competition for resources causes mortality among those least able to compete at all stages of life, but the rate of mortality is greatest after emergence, as juveniles disperse from the vicinity of the redds. Indeed, a typical stream in which millions of eggs were laid in early winter will support only tens of thousands of young fish by the late summer.

Growing and developing further, alevins become classed as fry after a month or so. In spite of their small size, fry move short distances upstream against the current, as well as longer distances downstream from where they emerge from the redd. In a small stream in the Aberdeenshire Dee, the movement of young fish away from an isolated redd was monitored. By late summer, fry could be caught up to 800m downstream and up to 200m above the redd's location. It seems probable that some alevins and fry are displaced much further downstream than this, especially in flood water. However, fish that will later survive do not seem to move in such a passive way. Sometimes, the pattern of dispersal of emerging fish must be quite complex because of competition between different families emerging from closely spaced redds. In any case, by summer, fry are living singly within restricted areas in the shallow parts of streams. These places are not favoured by the older parr and will have been abandoned by them as they grew in size. Fry continue to feed and grow in these places, becoming parr at some ill-defined point and moving to occupy territories in deeper or faster water.

A completed salmon redd in shallow water near the streamside. The water is flowing from right to left. The clean gravel in the foreground has been moved downstream to cover the eggs. The larger stones on the right proved too big for the female to move and they are lying in the pit left by the female's final bout of cutting.

In essence, each parr's feeding domain comprises two parts. Single parr have sole occupancy of a territory of 1 or 2 sq m. This territory lies within a more extensive area termed the home range. Parr occupying neighbouring territories exploit the resources of the home range jointly, but each attempts to defend the boundaries of its territory against intrusion by other fish. The mosaic of territories marked out with unseen boundaries on the stream bed is probably fairly fluid. Boundaries will inevitably change throughout the year as the extent of the stream bed and its geography alters with the seasons. Streams also change markedly from day to day with changes in rainfall or when freezing lowers their flow. Territories are vacated throughout the year as fish die for one reason or another and ultimately each parr vacates its final territory when it leaves fresh water for the sea. Vacancies will be occupied by other fish, especially younger fish, and perhaps by older parr previously in possession of an inferior domain. However, individuals attain some measure of territorial stability in spite of the unstable nature of streams and in spite of seasonal changes in the structure of the fish populations they support. Sometimes, indeed, the same parr can be found in roughly the same places over extended periods of time. The quality and the size of the territory that a fish is able to acquire will determine the value of the resources to which it has sole or privileged access. The resources each parr has at its disposal determine the course of much of its life.

A salmon parr lying motionless on the stream bed, showing the barred blue flank markings that characterise young fish. Salmon can be distinguished from trout because of the finer structure of their jaws and mouth and because their body is slimmer at its junction with the tail.

The benefits of living on familiar ground are many, and in most circumstances salmon parr remain in the same place. To hold position, they must move constantly against the current. This burden is not as heavy as it might seem however, since parr are seldom exposed to the full strength of the flow. Water velocity is slowest close to the stream bed because of friction between the flowing water and the substrate and because of turbulence set up near its rough surface. Parr spend most of their time here. Indeed, they are often at rest on the substrate, angling their large pectoral fins to the stream's flow. Viewing the activity of young salmon, the observer's main impression will be of economy of effort. Unless they are disturbed, parr restrict obvious activity to intercepting prey items passing in the drift and to making minor adjustments to trim.

The Girnock Burn smolt trap is built on the buttress of an old weir. In essence, it is a variable sieve that can be used to capture downstream migrants at any of a wide range of stream flows without causing the fish harm. Eight sections of sieve can be opened sequentially by removing the back-boards – only one section is operative in this photograph. Each section has removable horizontal boards that cover the parallel fibre-glass bars that constitute the sieve itself. Fish held back by the sieve pass to a channel of flowing water that delivers them to the holding box that is a prominent feature of the central foreground.

Falling leaves and flood water have inundated the Girnock Burn trap and those pictured are working to put it back into action.

The period of fresh-water growth lasts for at least a year. After that each fish is required to make decisions on a series of options that recur year by year with the seasons. Finally, each will become a smolt one spring and leave fresh water for the sea. But while some may become smolts at one year of age, most are older when they do so. The main determinant of the course that each fish adopts is growth and that, in turn, is determined largely by temperature. In the warm, productive rivers of southern Europe most fish become smolts at one year of age. In Arctic rivers many smolts are five or more years old. In Scotland, most smolts are two or three years old. The relationship between size and age at smolting is not a simple one, however, and smolts vary in length between about 100 and 200mm. Those fish that have grown most quickly become smolts in April or May, almost exactly a year after hatching, and the course of their lives will have been relatively straightforward until then. But it is two- or three-year-old smolts that occur most frequently in many streams and, for the males among them, life may well have been more complex. Many male parr become sexually mature and consort with adults at spawning time as we shall see later.

In spring, smolts differ in appearance from those of their brothers and sisters that remain parr. The latter are dark, cryptically coloured fish with spotted markings on the upper part of the body and barred blue flanks. In smolting fish this coloration becomes obscured, as the substance guanine is incorporated into the scales and gives the superficial silvered appearance that characterises the smolts. The fishes' behaviour also changes. Between April and June, smolts abandon their territories on the stream bed and their solitary mode of life to move downstream in small shoals. In some streams other fish of similar age and size will have left their territories some months before. These are the so-called autumn parr and they leave streams between September and November, spending the winter months lower in the river catchment before going to sea. Although autumn parr lack the silvering of smolts, they resemble them in other ways and might be considered pre-smolts.

A so-called precocious parr. The pronounced vertical banding is characteristic. Terming these parr 'precocious' suggests that they are unusual in some way. In fact, many male salmon become sexually mature without first migrating to the sea. Mature parr are fertile and they cover many of the eggs laid by sea-run females.

The processes involved in smolting are still a subject of conjecture, despite the numerous scientific studies carried out over many years. So great are the changes in appearance and behaviour accompanying smolting, that parr and smolts were formerly thought to be different types of fish and, by some, different species. It was always known that smolts were salmon, but they were considered to be the progeny of the adults that had spawned only six months before, becoming, according to Izaak Walton 'samlets in the spring next following'. Parr were held to be distinct in that they always stayed in fresh water. 'Skeggers, which abound in many rivers relating to the sea, are bred by such sick Salmons that might not go

Two young salmon lying side by side. Although these fish are not fully smolted, their barred markings have already become obscured by silvering.

to the sea'. Study of salmon reared in captivity placed the matter beyond doubt, but only in the mid-nineteenth century, when parr and smolts were finally shown to be different, normal stages in the life of a single species. Francis Day[1] gives a detailed account of this scientific controversy and the confusion surrounding it.

Perhaps the most important feature that distinguishes parr and smolts is that the latter acquire the ability to live in sea water. For parr, immersion in sea water leads quickly to death as a result, perhaps surprisingly, of dehydration. Sea water is a more concentrated solution of salts than the tissue fluids of salmon, and parr lose water across their body surfaces to the sea in the process known as osmosis. In fact all marine fish, including smolts, suffer in this way, but marine fish and smolts are capable of maintaining the water content of their own tissues by drinking large quantities of sea water and excreting the salt it contains. This ability to maintain body fluids in the face of the dehydrating effects of salt water is an essential component of the process of smolting. And smolting brings the resources of the open ocean within the reach of young salmon that have spent all their previous lives in the shelter of streams and rivers.

1. Francis Day. *British and Irish Salmonidae*, Williams and Norgate, London, 1887.

Wild smolts captured in the Girnock fish-trap in April. These fish are two or three years of age. The appearance of young salmon alters markedly as they change from parr to smolts. The dark coloured, barred and spotted parr become uniformly silver, owing to the deposition of the substance guanine on the surface of their scales. The fish change in many other ways too. Parr are bottom-living and resident. Sea water kills them. Smolts swim freely in open water, they migrate actively and they can live in the sea. As a general rule, the size of salmon streams and rivers controls the number of smolts they produce each year because each parr requires a living space of its own. On the other hand, large numbers of smolts can be reared at high density in tanks on farms. In Iceland, for example, five million smolts are released each year from salmon-ranching stations. When they return from the sea, ranched adults are harvested in the estuaries of the rivers where they were released.

The smolt trap constructed by the Canadian Department of Fisheries and Oceans on the Campbelltown River in Newfoundland. This is one of a number of research facilities intended to monitor the state of salmon populations after the moratorium on coastal netting imposed in Canada in 1992. The trap is a temporary structure that is installed each spring after the break-up of the winter ice. The structure comprises two diversion fences that span the river, linked by a central fish trap and holding box.

CHAPTER 2

Leaving for the Sea

As we have seen, parr are solitary creatures with a stationary mode of life. Their personal living space is small and as a consequence, their familiarity with it is total. In contrast, their appreciation of circumstances beyond their home range is at best incomplete. Information is limited to smells and signs carried downstream from above. Parr can know nothing of conditions downstream. Because of this lack of information, moving to seek new, better territory in more distant parts of a stream is attended by risks. And in general, parr living in adequate surroundings remain there, finding the uncertainties of moving elsewhere unattractive. When they become smolts, however, they prepare to explore far beyond the limits of their home range.

From the researcher's point of view, following the movements of the small fish poses special difficulties. Parr cannot easily be observed in streams and the range of activities they undertake is always diverse. Consequently, it is difficult to detect general patterns in the movements fish make or to reach general conclusions as to their causes. One solution has been to measure the movements of fish by constructing fish-traps. In this way it is possible to infer patterns of activity from patterns of capture, especially when trapping is total, when large numbers of fish are involved and when information is gathered over many years. Traps overcome many of the difficulties associated with gathering information on the migrations of salmon.

Since 1966, the Freshwater Fisheries Laboratory has operated two fish traps on the Girnock Burn, a spawning tributary of the River Dee in Aberdeenshire. One trap catches adults moving upstream and the other juveniles going downstream. In essence, the trap that intercepts the young fish takes the form of a variable sieve which separates fish moving down from the water in which they travel. The migrating fish are diverted to a holding box where they accumulate temporarily before being removed, examined, tagged and sent on their way downriver. By examining the average captures of fish moving downstream week by week over many years a broad pattern emerges. Two peak periods of capture occur: October and April. On average, about one third of all the fish which leave the stream each year do so in autumn and about two thirds in spring.

The Girnock Burn is typical of Scottish highland streams in that most young fish leave it when they are between about one and a half and three years of age.

Most autumn migrants leave the Girnock Burn one and a half or two and a half years after hatch. Most spring smolts are two or three years old. In warmer streams in southern latitudes, most fish leave after only one year. At the colder, northern latitudes, migration is sometimes deferred until the fish are five or more years old. Autumn migrants are more likely to be brothers or sisters of the smolts that emigrate the following spring rather than the previous one. So the migratory year can be considered as starting in autumn and finishing in spring. In the summer months, after the previous crop of migrants has left the Girnock Burn, the territorial mosaic is extremely stable and, as a result, none of the thousands of one- and two-year-old fish which still remain in the stream is captured at the trap. But even as the summer months decline, many of these fish have committed themselves to leaving the stream in the months that follow, as participants in the next annual migration.

Autumn parr start moving downstream in September. At this stage, they are still typically parr-like in appearance, showing none of the silvering that characterises spring smolts. Some of the parr captured in autumn have already become sexually mature. These are the so-called precocious males. Mature male parr are common in most salmon streams and they can be readily identified in September and October and especially in November, near to spawning time. Mature parr are characteristically overweight for their length and display unusually bold blue markings on their sides. In addition, light pressure applied to their flanks causes milt to be expressed from the vent.

When the patterns of capture of mature and immature parr are compared, it becomes clear that two separate migrations are taking place and for quite different reasons. Tagging studies show that the immature autumn migrants are moving purposefully towards the sea – in the van of the smolt migration. Strangely, it appears to take autumn migrants more than six months to reach the sea and it is presumed that they spend the winter within the river before becoming fully fledged smolts the next spring. The capture of mature parr reflects the movements these fish undertake in their attempts to reach and spawn with sexually mature adults. It can be shown that many mature parr are successful in this, as we shall see in Chapter 7. The forces driving the activity of mature parr can be inferred from their patterns of movement – and their patterns of movement can be deduced from their patterns of capture.

Mature parr are not found among the earliest autumn migrants, in spite of the ease with which they can be identified at this time. By October or November, mature and immature fish are being captured together. The difference in timing of the start of their movements to the trap is linked to the arrival of adult salmon. In October or November, adults that have lain in holding lies over the summer move into small streams like the Girnock Burn to spawn. This is of little significance to the immature parr but the presence of sexually mature adults stimulates activity among the small mature males. The spawning of adults begins in the Girnock Burn in the last days of October or in the first week of November. In those years when adults delay entering the stream until just before spawning time, mature male parr become active almost immediately. In other years, adults enter the stream several weeks before spawning and complete the process of sexual development in the stream itself. In these circumstances, the downstream movement of mature parr commences some time after the adults arrive. The movement of parr follows not from the presence of adult fish alone but from the presence of adults – and particularly females – which are becoming sexually active. The movements are local and driven by their attempts to locate and spawn with females.

Among sea-run males, large size and conspicuousness are the keys to dominance over competitors and dominance in turn is the key to sexual success. In an interesting paradox, male parr exploit their very lack of presence to achieve the same end. While adult males try to make an impression fairly and squarely, male parr operate the lesser gambit for sexual success known (in a piece of scientific humour) as sneaking. As the term suggests, sneakers are overlooked by large males because of the low profile they adopt. Escaping the aggressive displays directed by dominant males towards lesser adult males, some mature parr succeed in fertilising some of the eggs being shed by the females. As a rule, sneakers gamble for small wins compared with sea-run males. Individual parr are unable to fertilise many of the eggs shed by any female because of their size. Indeed many parr probably fail to gain access to spawning females at all, since they compete with each other much as adult males do. On the other hand, spawning parr play with small stakes too. The risks they take in becoming mature and attempting to spawn are low compared with the risks taken by fish which go to sea first. At the parr stage, for example, a relatively large proportion of the males have survived to attempt spawning. In contrast, many of the males that choose first to go to sea die there. In addition, parr retain the option of being able to spawn again in later years, either as parr once more or as adults. Most sea-run males die after their first spawning run.

The key to understanding the migrations of mature parr lies in a knowledge of the behaviour and physiology of the adult females as they near spawning. All the activities of the parr depend on what the adults do. Females choose the places where spawning will take place and the home ranges of most mature parr are always some distance away. To take any part in spawning, parr must leave their territories to follow females towards the spawning fords. Mature parr are drawn to passing females. The water-borne attractants (pheromones) which females secrete near spawning time act at long range. The presence of females in near-spawning condition breaks down the previously stable positions which mature parr have held in the territorial mosaic.

Of course, most parr move upstream towards females that have passed them, since they have no knowledge of how matters stand further downstream. But, as is usual in circumstances like these, matters are not clear cut and some downstream movements do also take place, as part of the same general increase in activity. This is why some mature parr are caught in the fish trap just before spawning takes place. But when these initial relocations are complete, a new stability is briefly established, and parr are not captured at the trap for several days just as spawning commences. Once spawning is under way and once the first adults have completed their redds, ripe males begin to leave the stream once more. This is the second phase of the downstream movement of mature male parr. The number of parr which take this new course depends on how many have succeeded in spawning. In years when few adult females enter the Girnock Burn, relatively few mature parr have the opportunity to spawn there and consequently many leave the stream to try their luck elsewhere. Conversely, in years when spawning adults are more numerous and more mature parr are able to spawn, fewer of them are captured at the trap. Participants in the second phase of the migration are by now genuine downstream migrants, seeking elsewhere the sexual success that has eluded them nearer their home ranges.

It seems clear then that much of the information that determines the movements of mature parr stems from the presence of the adults. Each year, however, mature parr living in the highest reaches of spawning streams, above the limits to which adult spawners penetrate, must make their decisions in the absence of much of the necessary information. In 1978, no adult salmon were allowed to pass beyond the Girnock fish-trap, and all the mature parr in the stream above the fish trap found themselves in the position experienced by only a few in other years. All of them were deprived of the usual cues for migration provided by adults. Shortly after the time at which spawning would usually have taken place, mature parr left the stream in greater numbers than ever before. The large numbers of migrants were attributable to the lack of opportunity for spawning experienced by all the mature parr in the stream that year. In the absence of other cues, the parr must be presumed to have based the timing of their movements on a knowledge of the passage of the autumn season and an appreciation of their own sexual condition. In short, these parr appeared to have retained all their options for as long as possible. When adults were still likely to arrive to spawn nearby, they waited near their home ranges. When adults failed to arrive, they left their home areas quickly, presumably to attempt spawning lower in the stream while they still remained near the peak of sexual condition.

The activity of the mature parr is designed to place them close to spawning females – wherever these are to be found – and the timing of their movements is intended to make the result most worthwhile. Indeed, these tactics and the sneaking which follows must often prove successful. Most redds contain some progeny sired by parr and in some redds the majority of the eggs have been fathered in this way.

Although, the movements of mature parr are of some interest, the fact remains that most of the young fish that leave streams are not sexually mature. Each year about 3500 migrants leave the Girnock Burn for the sea, either as autumn migrant parr or as spring smolts. Spring smolts occur in all salmon streams and as a result they have been well documented. Autumn migrants have not been so widely reported, although they probably go unnoticed in many streams and rivers among the floods and leaves of autumn. Smolts are accorded special status over autumn parr because of their changed appearance. However, the differences between the two are not as important as their similarities. Tagging studies show that both groups are leaving fresh water to go to sea and that both groups are equally successful in returning as adults.

Although the pressures which drive fish to migrate to the sea are not understood, the ultimate benefits of moving can be clearly identified. Successful reproduction is the final test of the success of fishes' lives. Those fish which journey successfully to the sea benefit from being able to exploit all its resources and they grow larger as a result. Large females benefit from being able to produce more eggs than small fish. Large males also benefit from having the edge over others as they compete for access to females at spawning.

As we have already seen, the earliest among the year's crop of migrants begin their journey from head-water streams in September; the last to leave do so in May. In spite of this, all young fish appear to reach the river mouth at about the same time in early summer. Some fish move rather rapidly and spring smolts tagged leaving the Girnock Burn have been caught as little as two days later by small boys fishing near Aberdeen, 80km downstream. Autumn migrants travel more slowly, apparently taking seven or eight months to make the same journey. The route to the sea is short for fish which have lived in streams near the coast and longer for those living in the higher reaches of major rivers. But again, fish from all parts of the same catchment reach the sea at about the same time of year by leaving their territories at different times and by moving downstream at different speeds.

The events leading up to migration can be thought of as being in two parts. First, resident fish become potential migrants as a result of internal changes that occur seasonally according to age and size. This process is known as priming. Primed fish are capable of migration but only do so when favourable conditions prevail. Among early migrants, the releasing stimuli must be strong but as time goes on primed migrants become less discriminating and ultimately primed fish move downstream anyway. In this way, migration is made fail-safe and by early summer all potential migrants have left their territories for the sea.

At the Girnock Burn, the main releasing factors are darkness and high flow. Almost all migrants travel the Girnock Burn under cover of darkness and in the first few hours after night has fallen. Their preference for darkness seems to extend to the night hours as well, since the moon's presence in the night sky reduces the number of fish captured in the trap. Moreover, many migrants travel on nights when the stream is swollen by rainfall. Indeed in autumn and in early spring, large floods are a prerequisite for migration. Later on, however, lesser floods suffice. As the fish become increasingly silvery, and as migratory activity becomes more intense, their requirements for special conditions in which to migrate diminish. The last migrants in spring will move downstream in low water flows and sometimes also by day.

Smolts can be observed now in daylight, swimming freely in clear water, sometimes in substantial numbers. They may be noticed in quiet pools in the loose shoals which have formed as passing smolts swept others onwards. Groups can be seen moving with the current, especially where they must pass through glides or still water. In other places, smolts may be observed to stem the river's flow, turning head upstream to control their passage through broken water. Of course, the shoals' final passage to the sea goes unseen; at this point the fish are temporarily lost from view.

The Faroese salmon-catcher *Sundaenni* berthed at Hvannasund in the northern Island of Bordoy in 1983. The Faroese salmon fishery was carried out between January and April each year, before the boats turned to fishing for other species. The salmon fishery was carried out in the ocean north of the islands. Catches there were of large multi-sea-winter salmon rather than the younger, smaller fish caught further south. Salmon were caught on hooks made up on floating long-lines, using sprats as bait. The fishery developed in the late 1960s and peaked in 1981 when landings exceeded 1000 tonnes. The fishery was restricted by quota in 1982 and suspended in 1991.

CHAPTER 3

The Lives of Adult Salmon

Once they leave fresh water, smolts can only rarely be observed or studied and consequently the next phase of their lives is almost undocumented. The number of smolts leaving fresh water may seem large (more than 10 million are estimated to leave Scottish rivers each year) but they are lost from sight in the sea and nothing is known of their migrations to the ocean feeding grounds.

At the end of October, 1978, a Faroese research vessel long-lined for salmon 65km north of Fugloy, the northernmost of the Faroe Islands. Some of the fish caught were in their first year at sea, having left fresh water only four or five months before. They were probably recent arrivals in the area. Although light for their length by comparison with older salmon, the incoming fish had grown considerably on their journey and were now more than 400mm in length. The country of origin of these fish, far less the rivers from which they had come, could not be known, of course. Salmon from the rivers of both eastern North America and Europe mix on the ocean feeding grounds (with the special exception of salmon from the Baltic rivers which confine their feeding to the Baltic Sea). Although mixing is far from uniform, fish from almost any river on the Atlantic coast of Europe might be caught in any of the fisheries in the northern Atlantic Ocean.

The extent of the ocean feeding areas of salmon are not fully known. Indeed, it is possible that this area of research has been deliberately neglected because of difficulties in regulating the fisheries that might result. In general terms, however, it appears that most salmon journey northwards to exploit the rich feeding along the so-called Arctic Front. This is a diffuse area of the ocean's surface where a mass of cold, nutrient-rich Arctic water flows south to meet the northward flow of the warmer North Atlantic Drift. Where these waters mix the ocean abounds with a great number of diverse marine species, and it is on these that salmon feed. Commercial fisheries for feeding salmon have existed in the past in the seas off western and southern Greenland, in Faroese waters and off the north Norwegian coast. It seems quite likely that the real distribution of feeding salmon extends between these areas and beyond them too, across a board tract of ocean of considerable size. The fishery off the north Norwegian coast was effectively closed in the mid-1970s. With the recent suspension of both the Faroese and the

A dip-net is used to secure a salmon caught on a floating long-line north of the Faroe Islands. This fishery is now suspended, although a small research fishery remains. A long-line may extend for more than 15km and bear 1000 or more hooks. The lines are set to fish overnight and hauled by day.

Greenland fisheries, no salmon are now caught in legitimate commercial fisheries in the distant oceans, although small research or subsistence fisheries do remain.

For a number of reasons, the high seas fisheries were pursued seasonally. From the biological point of view the most interesting reason is that the abundance of fish (and particularly the abundance of fish of marketable size) differs from place to place and changes throughout the year. Because of this the Faroese fishery was pursued in winter and the Greenland fishery in late summer. Changes in the distribution of salmon occur as they move into the feeding grounds for the first time and as they leave them. In addition, the geography of the oceans and of the feeding areas is not uniform. Salmon prey on other species which themselves depend directly or indirectly on planktonic organisms, and these are present in numbers that vary with location, with season and also from year to year. Unevenness in the distribution of these food species imposes patchiness in the distribution of the salmon that prey on them.

In the west Greenland fishery, floating drift nets were used to enmesh salmon making their way through the fjords and along the coast. In the Faroese fishery, salmon were caught on baited long-lines comprising many hundreds of hooks on 3 or 4m snoods spaced about 15m apart. The Faroese fishing grounds lie off the continental shelf, where the water is as much as 2000m deep, but the lines were set to float and salmon were caught only 1 or 2m below the ocean surface. The hooks were baited with sprats, a species that does not occur naturally in these northern waters. However, salmon have catholic tastes. In fact, they probably eat more or less anything of the right size that crosses their path and the contents of the stomachs of salmon caught in the fisheries contain a wide range of crustacean and fish species.

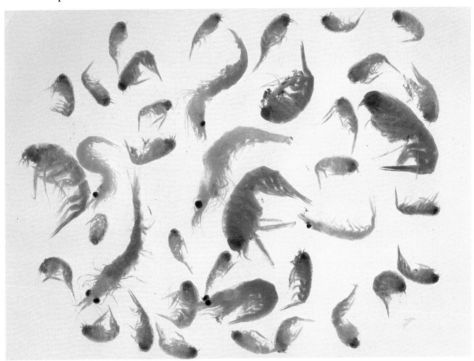

The stomach contents of salmon caught in Faroese waters. Several shrimp-like species of amphipod and euphausid crustacea (a major part of the salmon's diet) are represented here. They vary in size between about 5 and 20mm. Their brown-red colour is attributable to the carotenoid pigments which, in turn, impart the red colour to salmon flesh. In form and colour these food species are strongly reminiscent of some of the most popular salmon flies tied in small sizes.

John Hislop of the Marine Laboratory in Aberdeen examined the contents of 40 salmon stomachs taken from fish caught in late winter, 300km north of the Faroe Islands. The species they contained were identified, weighed and counted. Crustaceans (shrimp-like amphipods and euphausids) were most numerous overall, but fish (principally capelin, pearl-sides and lantern fish) formed the greater part by weight. In general, each salmon contained mixtures of fish and crustacean prey. Crustaceans are rich in the pigment astaxanthin, which gives the characteristic red flesh colour to salmon that feed on them. Some fish appeared to prefer particular prey species before their capture. For example, 10 of the 15 pearl-sides found in the 40 salmon examined had been eaten by one individual weighing 3.8kg. Together the pearl-sides weighed 4g. Some fish had expended considerable effort in catching small crustaceans. The greatest number were contained in the stomach of a 4.4kg fish that had consumed more than 1700 *Parathemisto* weighing 34g altogether. Bait sprats were present in the stomachs of only 12 of the 40 fish, presumably because most salmon did not swallow the bait before becoming hooked. However, two salmon contained two bait fish each and another contained three. These fish had evidently removed bait from the line without being hooked – at least until their last bite.

Salmon remain feeding at sea for a variable number of years before making their first – and often their only – return to fresh water. The number of years they have spent at sea can be seen by the patterns on their scales. The number of scales on a salmon is fixed and each scale must grow as the fish grows, to cover the expanding area of its body surface. They are built up at the edges in ring-like increments as the fish and their scales expand. In summer, when sea temperatures are high and growth is fast the rings are large. Winter rings are more closely spaced. The effect of this alternating pattern is to record the sequence of seasonal growth on every scale. Growth early in life is represented at the scale's centre and the most recent growth at its edge. Summers are shown by wide bands of large rings; winters by tight bands of smaller ones. The zone formed in sea water can be distinguished from the one formed earlier on in fresh water because sea growth in adults is so much faster than juvenile growth. This record of growth (and age) is permanent.

After feeding and growing in the ocean, salmon leave for home waters, prompted by the first stages of sexual development. At this stage their weights vary greatly – the smallest fish may weigh only 1.5kg while the largest may weigh more than 20kg. The key to where individuals lie on this scale is the length of time they have spent in the ocean. Many begin their return to home waters after feeding at sea for the shortest period possible – over the summer after entry to the sea, the following winter and for a part of the next summer. In some places, these small fish are numerous and they seem so easily distinguished from fish of greater sea age that they are accorded a special dignity: they are called grilse.

OPPOSITE

Salmon scales record patterns of growth. The lower part of the scale pictured in this photograph is the part that has protruded from the fish's flank. The upper part, which has been embedded in the skin, contains a complete record of the fish's lifetime growth. Scales grow at their edges by the addition of small, ring-like increments. The most recent rings are closest to the edge, and the earliest rings are embedded in the centre of the scale. Fewer, small rings are added in winter when growth is slow. More, larger rings are laid down in summer when growth is fast. Groups of small or large rings form alternate winter or summer bands. Growth is slower in fresh water than in the sea. The zone of fresh-water growth is therefore smaller than the marine zone. In the scale pictured here, the radius of the fresh-water zone is only about 20 per cent of the whole scale. The patterns on this scale show that it was from a fish that had spent three winters in fresh water and then two in the sea.

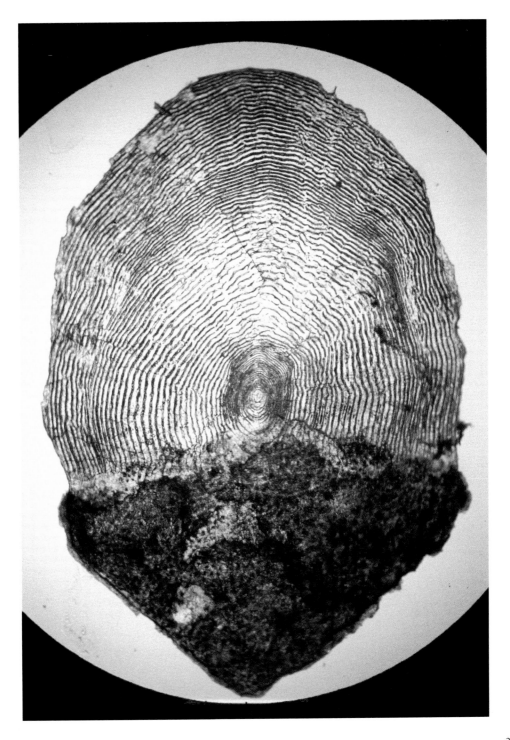

The essence of the grilse's life is that it leads to sexual maturity and spawning after only one winter in the sea. Some grilse appear on the coast and are caught in net fisheries as early as April, weighing around 2kg. Grilse arriving later will have fed for longer in the ocean and will weigh more. By the time the peak runs of grilse appear on the coasts their average weight is 3–3.5kg.

For some reason, grilse are deemed to be worth less than salmon in the commercial market. To make matters simple – at least where fish are being bought and sold – all fish caught in summer and weighing less than 8lb (3.5kg) have come to be classed as grilse. This rule of thumb has also been adopted by many anglers. However the rule is at best an approximation and it is not at all accurate for fish caught in late summer and autumn. Late-running grilse, caught as fresh fish towards the end of the angling season, may weigh 5kg or more.

When the grilse have left the ocean feeding grounds, the other fish remain there to continue feeding and growing without pause; they will leave the ocean later. Some will leave after only a further month or two, others will delay for a year or more. When fish like these spawn, the growth record on their scales will show two or more winter bands in the zone laid down at sea rather than the single band shown by spawning grilse. All these fish are classed as multi-sea-winter salmon, but unfortunately, this terminology is misleading in the case of those that return to fresh water first of all. The very first of the two-sea-winter (2SW) salmon leave the ocean before the second sea-winter actually starts. In some rivers, large late-running grilse moving quickly upstream near the end of the year are accompanied by the earliest-running of the 2SW salmon. At this stage, just like the grilse, the first of the 2SW fish will show only one winter band on the sea zone of their scales. Unlike the grilse however, the 2SW fish will pass another winter before they finally spawn a year or more later. The multi-sea-winter salmon's life is therefore better defined by the number of winters elapsing between smolting and spawning, not by the sea-age at which it returns to fresh water.

Although the future lives of the late-running grilse and the early-running 2SW salmon will be quite different, the fish may appear rather similar to the casual observer. What distinguishes the two groups with certainty is not their appearance (fresh-run grilse can still be well silvered, even late in the season) or their scales (both groups will bear rather similar patterns), but their sexual condition. By late autumn, all the grilse will have developed large ovaries or testes in preparation for spawning that year. In contrast, the reproductive organs of the 2SW salmon will remain small.

In the long run-up to spawning, early-running winter salmon will be joined by spring salmon and then by summer- and autumn-running salmon in turn. Having grown in the sea for a longer period, each successive class of fish will increase in average weight until autumn-running 2SW fish will average perhaps 6–8kg. So what of the largest fish? The British rod record salmon weighed about 30kg and 15–20kg fish are caught each year. These fish belong to the 3SW, 4SW and even older classes of fish that have lived and grown for much longer in the sea. Surprisingly perhaps, the largest salmon of all are always running to spawn for the first time. Debilitated by the demands of their first spawning, the few fish that return to fresh water for a second time are unable to add much to their previous weight.

The number of fish that return in the two principal classes – grilse and 2SW salmon – varies from year to year, probably as a consequence of changes in the environment experienced at sea. The sexes are not represented equally in either group: in general, males are more likely to be found among the grilse than among the multi-sea-winter salmon, and females dominate the older sea-age classes. Paradoxically however, the very largest, oldest sea-age fish are again males.

Salmon are already becoming sexually mature before their return to fresh water. This may seem surprising to anyone who has examined the reproductive organs of fish caught in rivers early in the season. At this time of year the organs of both males and females are much smaller than they are later in the season. However the reproductive organs comprise two parts. The reproductive products – milt or eggs – which finally constitute by far the larger part of the gonads develop almost entirely in fresh water, especially in early-run fish. In contrast, the unseen parts that secrete the hormones which hasten and control sexual development are active long before this. Sex hormones are already rising in some of the fish caught in winter on the ocean feeding grounds, a year or so before their first opportunity to spawn. The sex hormones exercise control over most aspects of biology, integrating the fishes' behaviour with their sexual development from the earliest stages of maturation until spawning itself. The return migration is the earliest external sign of the changes taking place within maturing fish.

Quite when the return migration starts or what form the early stages take are, of course, unknown. It seems unlikely that the transition between swimming within the feeding areas and coursing directly away from them is particularly abrupt. Instead the divergence is probably slow. Returning fish will intensify their homeward movements gradually, becoming clearly migratory some time after migration has actually started. As might be expected in fish that have abandoned the rich feeding areas they sought so assiduously before, returning fish lose their former preoccupation with feeding, and few of those netted close to the coast contain food. Not surprisingly, however, the abandonment of their former interests for new ones is not complete. Some salmon caught in coastal nets, especially in the earlier part of the summer, do contain food, and particularly sand-eels or herring.

The routes travelled in the ocean by salmon returning home are unknown, but as they approach the coasts our knowledge of them becomes more secure again. They can be followed, though still with difficulty, along the coasts and into the rivers and streams they left a year or more before. Salmon home with remarkable accuracy before they spawn. This important facet of their lives gives structure to all the others, as we shall see in the chapters that follow.

Finally, towards the end of the year, spawning brings the salmon's life-cycle to its conclusion. But even now the ultimate result of each life remains in doubt. Success at spawning is a crucial test of the success of each fish's life, but the final test is the future performance of their progeny – and so on, through the generations. Paradoxically perhaps, the life-cycle does not come full circle, since the structure of salmon populations changes continually from generation to generation. What finally remains of each generation at spawning differs from what existed at the very start. The lives of salmon are never quite the same and the cycles played out by individuals are never repeated exactly by their progeny. For the species, the circle is never closed. Life progresses in a sequence of open loops that spiral through the generations.

CHAPTER 4

The Return Home

At the most distant point in their journey through the northern oceans, salmon will have travelled hundreds or thousands of kilometres from their home rivers. The means by which they find their way home (and they do so almost unfailingly) are not fully understood, but they must use a variety of environmental cues as guide-posts at different stages on their journey. Many of the cues that seem likely to provide the necessary prompts are insubstantial and some change with the seasons. So salmon must handle the information they need for guidance with considerable skill.

On the first stage of their journey, from the ocean feeding grounds to the coastal shelf, the range of information available appears slight. Land is distant and much of the journey is made where water of great depth lies over the sea-bed contours. Navigation here cannot be based on a knowledge of the physical geography of the continental land masses or the ocean floor. Fish are aware of the surface features of the ocean, and temperature, salinity and current speed and direction probably vary enough to offer some guidance. But in general, these sources of information seem too fickle, too slight or too imprecise to offer a reliable basis on which to steer the course home. The crucial information must be culled from sources other than these.

By a process of elimination, it appears likely that salmon in the open ocean will be found to rely (as seafarers have done in the past) on the cues provided by the Earth's magnetic field or by the day- or night-sky. Orientation may be based on any or all of these features and precise navigation can be achieved if salmon are capable of assimilating the information they require. The sun's position in the sky perhaps provides the most obvious and straightforward directional guidance. But the possibilities afforded by compass navigation using the Earth's magnetic field ought also to be recognised.

Although humans have no sense of the existence of magnetic fields, it has become clear that many species of animals do, and salmon may well be among them. In particular, iron is a common constituent of the body tissues of all vertebrate animals. In some species it is present in the form of the mineral magnetite which, when unrestrained, has the physical property of aligning with magnetic fields. It can be imagined how magnetite, embedded and restrained in a tissue matrix, might generate the signals that make animals aware of their

A jumper-net set on the sand beaches north of Aberdeen. The helicopter in the background is returning from the off-shore oil production platforms in the North Sea – a contrast between traditional and the new methods of exploiting the sea's resources. Jumper-nets have been operated for more than 100 years and they follow an even older design. Each net comprises a leader set towards the shore and anchored near the high-tide mark. This is coupled to an inscaled head or trap supported on stakes and moored to wooden pins set into the sand. Jumper-nets fish over the tide and they are emptied twice daily, as the tide recedes but before the nets become dry.

magnetic alignment, particularly in relation to the Earth's magnetic field. In salmon, microscopic particles of magnetite have been identified in a number of body tissues and particularly in the tissues along the length of the lateral line[2]. Perhaps these arrays are the basis of a sense that permits magnetic orientation and compass navigation.

Good experimental evidence for compass navigation by salmon is lacking, and to examine the matter further it is necessary to look elsewhere among migratory

2. A. Moore, S.M. Freake and I.M. Thomas. 'Magnetic particles in the lateral line of the Atlantic salmon (*Salmo salar* L.)'. *Philosophical Transactions of the Royal Society of London*, Series B (1990) 329: 11–15.

species. Loggerhead turtles for example, face all the navigational problems that salmon do in making their own transatlantic round trip. The loggerheads' journey lasts for several years and takes them to the southern Atlantic coasts of Europe from the Caribbean and Florida beaches where they hatch – and where, eventually, they return to breed.

Recent experiments[3] have shown how loggerheads use an awareness of the Earth's magnetic field to help steer their course. Each loggerhead's compass is set at the very beginning of its life as it leaves the beach after hatching and heads eastwards into the sea. This compass alone would be sufficient to enable it to continue holding an eastwards course across the Atlantic. But the basic compass appears to be backed up by a more sophisticated accessory that allows it to sense its latitudinal position. The angle that the Earth's magnetic field bears to the Earth's surface changes with latitude. Loggerheads appear to be aware of this and are therefore able to judge the north–south aspect of their eastwards course. Thus loggerhead turtles, at least, are capable of sensing, interpreting and using the navigational cues offered by the Earth's magnetic field to help them make a long circuit through the ocean. Perhaps salmon can also do this.

By whatever means salmon acquire the information they need for navigation, its processing must be complex. Thus, at critical stages in their journey, salmon that have previously lived together must plot different courses using the same information. For example, fish from the western and eastern Atlantic rivers mix on the west Greenland feeding grounds, as we saw in Chapter 3. At some point, the return journeys of these two broad groups must diverge to take generally southerly or easterly headings. The simplest possible explanation for differences like these is that salmon base their return course through the ocean on some memory of their outward journey. But complex compensatory shifts would be necessary to do this unless the salmon's return journey retraces the exact route of the outward one, which seems unlikely. Further, if navigation is based on seasonally changing features, such as the sun's position in the sky, additional compensation will be necessary to allow for the passage of the seasons between the outward and inward journeys.

While salmon undoubtedly rely heavily on prompts from the outside world, it appears likely that some of the information necessary for the return journey resides permanently within each fish. The journey may be based in part, on a racial memory stored in the genes. Bams[4] has shown that a mechanism like this exists among pink salmon on the Pacific coast of Canada. Working on the Tsolum River in British Columbia, in which natural runs of pink salmon had been depleted, Bams compared the performance of pure stock imported from the Kakweiken River (about 160 km away) with crosses between imported Kakweiken fish and the few remaining Tsolum fish available for breeding. Bams introduced fry of both groups into a tributary of the Tsolum River, after marking them so that both groups might be identified and distinguished later on their return from the sea. When the adult fish did return, Bams compared the rates at which the two groups were caught in the commercial fishery along the coast and finally in the Tsolum River itself.

3. K.J. Lohmann and C.M.F. Lohmann. 'Acquisition of magnetic directional preference in hatchling loggerhead sea turtles'. *Journal of Experimental Biology* (1994) 190: 1–8.
4. R.A. Bams. 'Survival and propensity for homing as affected by presence or absence of locally adapted paternal genes in two transplanted populations of pink salmon (*Oncorhynchus gorbuscha*)'. *Journal of the Fisheries Research Board of Canada* (1976) 33: 2716–25.

Both groups of adults returned to the coastal fishery in similar numbers, showing that similar numbers had survived. But the number of Kakweiken-Tsolum crosses found later in the Tsolum River was much greater than the number of pure Kakweiken fish found there. The crosses made their way into the river, and especially towards the tributary where they had been released, in greater numbers than the pure imported stock. In other words, even half-native fish were able to make their way back to and through the Tsolum River with greater facility than non-native fish. Part of the capacity for accurate homing was contained in the genes that distinguish the pink salmon of the Tsolum and Kakweiken Rivers.

The most curious aspect of what Bams discovered is that the genetic differences that he was able to detect were so telling so near to the end of the fishes' journey. Migrants would be expected to rely most heavily on any genetic guidance systems they may possess before this stage because alternative, environmental cues for navigation are likely to be sparse when the fish are distant from the coast. In spite of this, however, the Kakweiken fish and the Kakweiken-Tsolum crosses proved equally adept at making their way back to the coast from the ocean.

Of course, the Tsolum and Kakweiken Rivers are separated by only about 160km. On this small geographical scale, both groups of fish may have performed adequately in spite of slight intrinsic differences in their navigation. The navigational problems posed for many Atlantic salmon are much more testing than those posed for Bams' fish. In the extreme case, as we have seen, North American and European salmon must find their way back to the opposing Atlantic coasts from the same northern feeding grounds. Perhaps, like loggerhead turtles, Atlantic salmon use a magnetic sense to enable them to make these decisions. Perhaps, as in loggerheads, the compass is set as salmon make the outward journey towards the feeding grounds.

It is also possible, however, that the compass is permanently set in the genes. This proves to be the case in the blackcaps, a migratory warbler that spends the winter period and the summer breeding season in different parts of Europe. Since about 1960, a new, winter population of blackcaps has become established in Britain. This has resulted from genetic change in the blackcap population that breeds in Bohemia in central Europe. The blackcaps that will over-winter in Britain show a strong tendency to adopt a westerly heading in autumn, when they begin their migration from Bohemia. This contrasts sharply with the southerly heading adopted by those birds that will spend the winter in the traditional manner in the Mediterranean. The difference between birds that over-winter in Britain and those that migrate to the Mediterranean is heritable. Young birds that have no experience of the journeys involved adopt the magnetic compass headings passed to them in their parents' genes.

The tendency of some blackcaps to migrate westwards in autumn has arisen spontaneously as a result of random genetic change. Indeed, changes of the same type probably occur all the time and they probably occur in other migratory species, too. Blackcaps over-wintering in Britain have been successful since 1960 (but possibly only as a result of the increased provision of food on bird-tables).

In the past, the greater part of the salmon catch has always been made by the commercial rather than the sports fisheries. In 1960, about 7000 tonnes of wild Atlantic salmon were caught world-wide. In 1993, the corresponding figure was 3500 tonnes. In Europe, the catch dropped from 5500 to 3000 tonnes over the same period. Catches have declined for a number of reasons. Many commercial fisheries have been terminated, suspended or restricted by legislation, by agreement or because they ceased to be viable. The reduced abundance of salmon in the seas has been a factor in each case.

And in spring, British birds prove themselves able to return to the traditional breeding areas in central Europe. Often, however, new migrations will bring blackcaps (or other migratory species) to locations that cannot support them or from which they cannot return. Migrants like these will die, and their genes will die with them. However, the new genes that British blackcaps carry have been tried and tested by Nature over 30 years and have proved viable so far.

There is one further twist in this tale. It is unlikely that the two migratory routes are equally favourable to the birds. Young blackcaps inherit genes from both parents. If birds that were genetically predisposed to migrate westwards interbred with those programmed to move south, the more favourable lifestyle and the better genes would soon come to dominate among blackcaps generally. And as a consequence, the new route or the old one would be abandoned. It is probable, however, that the two migratory types of blackcap do not interbreed freely. Experiments suggest that British birds return to the breeding grounds about 10 days before Mediterranean ones. If this is the case, British birds will form into breeding pairs before the Mediteranean birds arrive, and the latter will pair later among themselves.

These studies of blackcaps[5] illustrate two further noteworthy points that we will return to later: how spontaneous genetic change enables migratory animals to exploit new situations and how reproductive isolation and lack of competition foster the maintenance of new genetic traits. But in the contexts of migration and navigation, these studies have demonstrated the importance of the genes in determining orientation – among blackcaps, at least.

By whatever means salmon navigate, it would be surprising if they proved capable of returning through the open ocean to the coast with exceptional accuracy. And indeed, fish heading for Scottish rivers appears to reach the coast along a broad front. As the coast nears, the range of possible cues for direction-finding increases. Visual cues are an obvious possibility but the indirect effects of the coast's physical presence are important too. For instance, low-frequency sound is capable of travelling through water for substantial distances. The noise generated by waves beating on the shoreline is probably audible at some distance. Perhaps this affords a means of orientating with the shoreline even when it is beyond sight. Interestingly, in a study of acoustically tagged salmon moving in coastal water several kilometres offshore, the fishes' movement relative to the water in which they were swimming (allowing for the direction and speed of the tides) always showed a strong onshore tendency.[6]

Indeed, the capture and release of marked fish suggests that coastal geography plays a major role in guiding fish in the later stages of their journey through the sea. For many years, salmon captured in fisheries around the Scottish coast have been tagged and released to continue their journey. Some of these fish have been captured again later, in rivers and in coastal fisheries elsewhere. A composite pattern of movement can be pieced together from information gathered over the years. Fish returning to Scottish rivers appears to follow the coastline along either of two main tracks. One approaches from the west, taking fish up the west coast,

5. P. Berthold, A.J. Helbig, G. Mohr and U. Querner. 'Rapid microevolution of migratory behaviour in a wild bird species'. *Nature* (1992) 356: 668–670.
6. A.D. Hawkins and G.W. Smith. 'Radio-tracking observations on Atlantic salmon ascending the Aberdeenshire Dee'. Scottish Fisheries Research Report No. 36 (1986).

along the north coast and south through the Moray Firth towards the Aberdeenshire coastline. The other approaches from the south-east, sweeping northwards along the east coast, again towards the Aberdeenshire rivers. As they pass by, salmon leave these tracks along the way to enter rivers scattered along the coast.

Salmon moving along the coastline are caught surprisingly near to shore. Of course, this is partly because the nets used to catch them are set there. On the other hand, the nets are set where experience gained by netsmen over many years has shown that they are most effective. The fixed stake-nets used on sand beaches on the Scottish east coast are set using leader nets stretching over part of the shore between the high and low-water marks. On neap tides, shallow nets may fish only a small section of the beach stretching less than 50m from the high-water mark. In spite of this, these nets still catch salmon that are moving through surf, in water that is sometimes only about a metre in depth.

At some point near the end of their journey through the seas, returning salmon cross the path they followed on the outward migration a year or more before. At this point they enter familiar ground, gaining access to signs and signals that they have experienced previously. Indeed, experimental studies suggest that their journey into and through fresh water is guided by local knowledge and based on the process known as sequential imprinting. In this process, juveniles accumulate a sequence of permanent memories during their migration downstream. As adults, they recall these memories in reverse order, to guide them back to their original locations. The rapidity with which these memories are formed and the permanence with which they are retained pay startling tribute to the salmon's mental capacity. As fish near their home rivers on their journey along the coast, they switch from the general navigational headings they have used in the open seas to accurate headings based on imprinted local information.

In making their journey along and around the coasts, salmon pass repeatedly through fresh water discharging from rivers. Fresh water is less dense than sea water and tends to spread across the surface of the sea. Plumes of river water exist separately for some distance before wave action and the movement of the tides mixes them thoroughly with the sea. For example, satellite pictures show that the plume of the River Shannon, Ireland's largest river, sometimes extends as far as 65km out to sea. It is supposed that salmon test river plumes using their sense of smell to discriminate their own river from others. Geology and vegetation may impart characteristically different odours to different river waters. However, Nordeng[7] has proposed that it is the fish themselves that engender the differences: that returning fish can detect and respond to specific odours produced by juvenile members of the population to which they belong.

However, discrimination is apparently not wholly accurate, and mistakes are made. For instance, some of the fish tagged leaving the Girnock Burn as smolts are caught when they return to fresh water. In the years between 1967 and 1980, 126 tagged salmon were caught on the River Dee itself. Surprisingly perhaps, 63 were caught in other rivers nearby. As might be expected, (recalling the route that fish

---

7. A. Nordeng. 'Is the local orientation of anadromous fishes determined by pheromones?' *Nature* (1971) 233: 411–413.

Otters number salmon among the species they prey on.

appear to take along the coast), most of the fish caught outside the Dee were reported from the nearest river to the south, the North Esk. Some of the findings of Bob Laughton's study of salmon movements in the River Spey[8] suggest that the mistakes made by Dee fish would have been rectified before long. Of 69 salmon radio-tagged as they entered the Spey, 12 were recorded leaving the river later. Most of these fish had remained in the Spey for a week or more and most had moved upriver for more than 20km during this time. One of them was caught later by an angler in the River Findhorn about 30km along the coast.

Having identified the river that they will first run, salmon may enter it or they may delay. Occasional casual reports exist of large aggregations of salmon lying offshore. At other times, large numbers congregate in estuaries. In some places it is possible to observe waiting fish moving back and forth on the tides, and in others continual leaping gives their presence away. When fish do commit themselves to entering fresh water their behaviour is not at all tentative. The extent to which they penetrate fresh water and the speed with which they do so vary greatly, but typically the first burst of swimming in fresh water lasts for several hours and takes fish several kilometres upstream. Upstream movement continues regularly for several days afterwards, usually in the hours of darkness, until the fish settle in their initial place of residence. At this stage the first phase of their run is complete.

8. Robert Laughton. 'The movements of adult Atlantic salmon (*Salmo salar L.*) in the River Spey as determined by radio telemetry during 1988 and 1989'. Scottish Fisheries Research Report No. 50 (1991).

Salmon are vulnerable in small streams. This spawner – a male – has been removed from the stream, killed and partially eaten by an otter. The carcase may well be visited again.

Salmon remain resident in their first locations for periods of weeks or even months. This is the second phase of their life in rivers. Radio-tracking studies show that places of residence are often in major pools, in sheltered, deep and undisturbed water. During their period of river residence, fish may occasionally move to new positions, usually further upstream. The intervening distance is covered in another journey lasting for hours or for a day or two. This is often made up of a number of shorter journeys, separated by periods of rest. Eventually, activity stops completely as before, and the fish becomes resident in a new location. The extent of the reduction in the fishes' movements during residence is so great that it is often difficult to comprehend. Indeed, even experienced field-workers have sometimes doubted that they were monitoring fish at all, believing that the signals they were locating were being emitted by loose tags cast by fish that had moved on. In cases like these, close examination of the exact position of the source of the signals often shows minor movements and the researcher's persistence is rewarded when the fish moves on.

The pattern of movement that takes fish to and from their resident lies has been examined in a number of studies carried out in different rivers, on different sea-age classes and different times of year. On the whole, the general pattern of movement is the same wherever it is studied. On the other hand, considerable variation exists in the patterns of movement shown by individual fish. This can be attributed to a number of factors that affect the extent to which fish adhere to their planned itineraries. For example, low river flows or low temperatures impede progress, leading to delays. High flows facilitate movement at all times and often appear to reinitiate upstream migration among fish that have been lying dormant in the same lies for some time.

Not all the causes of this variation are extrinsic. The condition of the fish changes as the season passes. Sexual maturation is the driving force behind upstream migration and the sexual condition of fish differs throughout the year and throughout the run. Sometimes fish appear tentative in the early stages of the migration. Forays upstream where main river-stems branch or into smaller tributaries are often not followed through. Salmon stack up in junction pools on major rivers and these often provide angling of exceptional quality until the fish move on. The sense of smell is one of the main sources of information for homing and sensitivity increases with sexual development. So the exploratory probings evident early in the run are probably made by fish that are not yet able to pinpoint their way with confidence. Indeed, the straying that occurs between rivers is probably the earliest sign of exploration by fish operating at the limits of their ability to discriminate their target river from others. Later, as time passes, behaviour becomes more focussed and the final run to the spawning redds is made quickly and directly.

Individuals change through the season but at all stages they also differ markedly from one another. Above all else, the extent and the timing of their movements are conditioned by homing. Fish run rivers to take up residence near to the places where they will spawn, but below them. The earliest-running fish spawn highest in the rivers and the latest-running ones nearest to the sea. It follows that the distance that they run into rivers also varies with the season. On average, early-running fish run farther than late-running ones to take up residence in their final lies.

In many rivers, the situation is more complex even than this. The grilse and 2SW salmon classes often differ in the times at which they run. In particular, grilse enter rivers only in summer and autumn. Where spring-running fish occur, they will already have been resident for several months before the first grilse arrive. In rivers like these, the first grilse heading for the furthest reaches of the river make their way upstream together with summer-running 2SW salmon. These summer salmon are late arrivals among the river's 2SW class. They have their sights set lower in the river than the spring-run fish that have preceded them, and lower too than the earliest-running grilse. In these circumstances, the relationship between time of entry and distance travelled is still present but it is obscured by differences between the sea-age classes.

In late autumn, near spawning time, residence ceases and fish enter the third phase of their run: the final surge to the spawning grounds. This journey is quite brief for those fish that spawn in the gravel beds of the main river. The journey through tributary streams to the highest reaches of catchments is more arduous. Most of our knowledge of the biology of salmon near spawning time has been gained by studying fish in tributary streams, as the difficulties of working in large rivers during autumn and winter make most types of study there impracticable. Even in small streams, gathering information is a formidable task for those involved. The difficulties that the fish themselves must overcome are no less.

In general, small tributary streams are not an ideal habitat for adult fish. Large salmon in small streams are highly vulnerable to predators because of insufficient cover and space for manoeuvre. In fact, otters target small streams at spawning time as sources of accessible, easy and substantial prey, and some fish are killed before and during spawning. On the other hand, tributaries are among the most productive areas of river catchments and the progeny of tributary spawners do well by comparison with juveniles spawned elsewhere. As a result, salmon go to considerable trouble to spawn in small streams, accepting the associated risks.

CHAPTER 5

Patterns of Return

It is commonly believed by anglers that sexual maturity follows the return to fresh water rather than preceding it. But, as we have seen, salmon return from the sea because they are already becoming mature. The hormones which initiate and control sexual development are raised in all salmon entering rivers, as they have been for some time before. The sex hormones begin to take charge while salmon are still far out at sea.

Hormones are extremely powerful substances. Their presence even in tiny concentrations affects all the body's functions. The levels of sex hormones in spring-running salmon are between 1 and 5 nanograms per millilitre of blood. (A nanogram is a one thousand millionth part of a gram). Even these tiny amounts of hormone are sufficient to induce the changes that bring salmon back to the rivers. Much later on, near full sexual maturity, hormone levels have increased but they are still less than 100 nanograms per millilitre. By this stage, the hormones have caused spawners to change both their appearance and their behaviour. In both these respects, the sexes have ceased to be similar. Male and female hormones are different substances and, in most respects, they have quite different effects.

Rivers differ greatly in supporting different types of fish. Most of the larger rivers have runs of both grilse and 2SW salmon. But in some smaller rivers the runs are composed almost entirely of grilse. In most rivers nearly all the salmon die after spawning for the first time, but in some repeat spawners are more common. Fish enter most of the major Scottish rivers every month of the year. However, their numbers vary considerably and the runs peak at different times in different rivers. In the past, it was not possible to be precise about numbers, but in future the increasing development of electronic fish-counters will change this. In the meantime, the patterns in which fish enter rivers cannot be determined. They can only be deduced from the rates at which they are caught.

OPPOSITE
The Terra Nova River in Newfoundland. The river splits into two parts above the point from which this photograph was taken. Both streams reunite in the middle distance where a jet of spray on the right marks an impassable vertical fall. A pass on the main stream allows salmon to reach the upper catchment.

Catches are an imperfect measure of patterns and numbers, particularly since the fishing seasons cover only a part of the year. Even so, the general character of the fisheries of the Nith in south-western Scotland, for example, and the Dee in the north-east can be shown to differ markedly. Early-season fishing on the Nith is not notable and the river fishes best late in the year. In fact, the Nith season closes last in Scotland in recognition of the unusual lateness of its runs. The Dee, on the other hand, is a spring river where fresh 2SW salmon are present in considerable numbers on the first day of February when angling commences. In a wider context, southern and mid-Europe's spring-fishing rivers have no counterpart in Scandinavia or North America.

Differences in the character of fisheries tend to persist over the years. However, the overall proportion of fish returning in the various sea-age classes changes from year to year and it changes cyclically too, over periods of many years. The underlying reasons are complex but they probably result, in part at least, from changes in the quality of life on the ocean feeding grounds. In years when marine life is abundant and feeding is good, fish tend to be larger than usual for their sea age and marine survival is high. In seasons when the grilse are large they tend to be numerous in the fisheries. Since many of the grilse die after spawning they are lost as potential members of the following year's run of 2SW salmon. Obviously, the numbers of 2SW salmon must therefore reciprocate to some extent with the number of the previous year's run of grilse. On the other hand, good runs of grilse often presage good runs of 2SW salmon for the following year. As a rule, when the fish do well at sea, the effects of high survival tend to swamp all the other effects and both the grilse and the 2SW fisheries prosper.

Of course, variations in the relative numbers of fish returning at any sea age are of great importance to the angler. In general, 2SW salmon are larger than grilse and the sea age composition of the catch affects its average size. Moreover, sea age is one of the factors that determines when fresh fish will be present in rivers since, as we have seen, the timing of the return migration is different in grilse and in older salmon.

Because of their short life at sea, grilse have to compress their sexual development into a relatively short time. As a result, the return migration is similarly compressed. Older salmon take longer over the whole process of maturity and they can exercise a more varied range of options for their return. In consequence, many of the 2SW salmon enter rivers earlier than all the members of the grilse class. The earliest-running 2SW salmon enter fresh water a year or more before they will spawn. Greater numbers follow in spring and summer and 2SW fish continue to enter rivers until just before spawning time. The grilse have fewer options and few are ready to leave the sea for fresh water until the end of May. The main grilse runs are in summer and autumn but, like 2SW salmon, they continue to enter rivers until spawning time. These late-running grilse have been at sea for as much as five months longer than the early ones. Consequently they are much larger and they are often classed in error as 2SW fish.

Overall, the majority of salmon enter rivers in the summer and autumn. The early-running 2SW salmon found in spring are relatively few in number but their

The salmon pass on the Terra Nova River. The passway has been engineered to baffle and break the strength of the flow. A series of interlinked pools has been constructed to break the fishes' journey and to provide areas of slack water where running fish may rest as they move through.

commercial and sporting value makes them worthy of special attention. Typically, winter- and spring-running fish occur in the larger rivers of the southern part of the European range. Rivers like the Dee and the Wye, for example, are still noted for the quality of their spring fishing, in spite of recent (and perhaps temporary) declines in the numbers of spring fish being caught. There are generally no spring-running fish in northern Europe and North America. Winters are severe there and the first runs do not take place until May or June, after the spring thaw. However, the earliest of all runs of salmon take place on some of the most northern of the European rivers. These fish enter fresh water before the beginning of winter and considerably more than a year before spawning. It seems they pass the winter lying below the river-ice.

In spite of differences between rivers, radio-tracking of migrating fish shows that order does exist within single catchments. As we have seen, the earliest-running 2SW fish spawn furthest from the sea and those entering later spawn lower down. A similar pattern can be discerned separately among the grilse, in spite of the compressed nature of their return migration. The earliest of the grilse run several months after the earliest of the 2SW salmon but both groups finally spawn in the same locations. Later in the season, the time gap between the sea-age classes closes, and the latest entrants of both classes run together to spawn in the lowest reaches of rivers, closest to the sea.

For the river manager, the strengths of the seasonal components of the fishery indicate the size of the spawning stock to be expected later in various parts of the catchment. For the angler, patterns of return dictate when and in what numbers salmon may be expected to occur. In addition, time of river entry is determined by the distance fish intend to travel before spawning. So the times at which fish enter a river might be expected to determine how they will be distributed along its length. As a general rule, early entrants are present for more of the angling season in the upper beats; later entrants are caught only lower down.

Early in the season, however, the expected pattern cannot be discerned. Salmon are cold-blooded, lacking the ability to regulate their body temperature. The biochemical processes that produce energy from the body's reserves are slowed at low temperatures, so the fishes' ability to generate power is reduced in the early part of the season and cold water slows upstream progress. As a result, early entrants often stack up temporarily in the lower reaches of rivers, moving freely only when temperatures rise.

When rivers do become warmer, the expected patterns of distribution begin to emerge and as time passes they become clearer. Of course anglers are aware of this and it is often remarked that rivers fill with fish from the top down. As a general description this statement is correct, but the implication that fish file into rivers, forming passively into orderly queues, is not sound. On the contrary, salmon determine the locations they will target for spawning while they are still juveniles, before they leave fresh water for the sea. Long before spawning time, they manoeuvre for access to their target locations by striving to reach holding pools just short of their final destinations. This is part of the process of homing.

It has been known since Walton's day that salmon home. What is not generally recognised, even now, is that homing within rivers is highly accurate. Dick Saunders of the Department of Fisheries and Oceans in Canada first showed this by following adult fish that had been tagged as juveniles through a series of fish traps on the Northwest Miramichi River in New Brunswick. Fish that had been tagged higher in the river penetrated greater distances upstream on their return as adults.

The confluence of the Girnock Burn (flowing from the right of the photograph) and the River Dee. The stream carries less than one per cent of the river's flow. Yet many adults, tagged in the stream as juveniles, are able to make their way back there after an absence of one or two years in the ocean. Adult salmon make use of memories laid down on their journey downstream to make the return journey. The nature of the cues that adults use to pinpoint their way are a matter of conjecture.

Taking this point further, the Girnock Burn is a small tributary stream in the middle reaches of a complex catchment drained by a large river. The stream's small size and its remote location might be thought to pose insuperable problems for fish attempting to find their way back there. Yet tagging studies show that about half the adults captured by the Girnock Burn fish-trap have lived in the stream above the trap as juveniles. Indeed, this figure probably underestimates the real extent of homing because the Girnock trap spans the stream at a single point on its length.

The Girnock Burn fish traps at summer flow. The smolt trap is visible in the background. In the foreground is the diversion fence of the adult trap. The fence is embedded in a concrete plinth. The vertical bars are close enough to prevent even small adult salmon passing through. The spacings are also too small to prevent baulked fish becoming gilled as they probe the gaps. The fence is sufficiently high to accommodate most of the range of stream flows that occur. At the very highest flows, adult fish can pass over the fence. However, they are prevented from moving further upstream by the rampart of the smolt trap and they can be recovered between the traps when the flood water passes. The fence is positioned obliquely across the direction of the stream's flow to lead ascending fish into the closed holding box built into the stream bank. Once salmon enter the holding box they are prevented from leaving by a V-shaped inscale on the entry slot and the fish can be recovered later for examination.

The dimensions of the homing units to which fish return are unknown but it is extremely improbable that the position of the fish-trap coincides by chance with the lower boundary of the Girnock homing unit. Because of this we must imagine that each year tagged adults go uncaptured near to but below the fish-trap. These fish will have stopped some way short of their exact juvenile position but may well consider themselves to be within the boundaries of the homing unit. In the same way, untagged adults that lived as juveniles near to but below the trap will be captured by it as they overshoot their juvenile positions to penetrate higher in the homing unit than before.

Above the fish-trap, the precision that homing fish achieve must be less than the entire length of the stream (about 10km). On average of course, the precision with which these fish home is likely to be rather less than this distance. This is a remarkable achievement at the end of a journey through the oceans lasting for a year or more and reckoned (even as the crow flies) in thousands of kilometres. Further, since fish appear to be capable of homing with a degree of precision that is less than the Girnock Burn's length, it is possible that some of them home not only to the stream, but to particular parts of it as well. Unfortunately there are no practical means of describing the dimensions of homing units or their shapes. The ways in which homing units relate to each other and to the geography of rivers are also unknown.

On the other hand, it is possible to begin to consider how large or small population groupings are. Thus, about 3500 migrants are trapped and marked at the Girnock Burn each year as they make their way downstream. Later, about half of the adults returning to the Girnock fish-trap show these marks. The extent to which unmarked fish dilute the marked ones tells us how many fish belonged to the Girnock population group as a whole at the time when marking was carried out. It follows that the whole Girnock population comprises the 3500 migrants produced in the 10km of stream above the trap and another 3500 migrants produced somewhere below it. The geographical dimensions of the Girnock population unit cannot be deduced from this information – it may be very compact or its downstream edge may be very diffuse. Numerically, however, the Girnock population is quite small. Its 7000 members comprise only a very small proportion of the many migrants produced by the whole Dee catchment.

It is not at all clear why fish that run in winter and home to the highest spawning locations adopt this particular style of life. Early-running 2SW salmon take more than a year to complete their journey through fresh water. Early-running grilse accomplish the same journey in six months. Yet both classes appear to be capable of making their journey in days. One might wonder why fish like these stop feeding in the sea so much sooner than seems necessary. Fish go to sea to feed heavily and grow quickly. But in returning so soon, early-running fish appear to fail to follow this through. For example, 2SW salmon that run rivers in early spring are only about half the size of those that run in late autumn. Grilse running in June are a kilogram or two lighter than those running in October. Body weight is an important factor in determining success at spawning and the penalties that early-running fish incur therefore seem clear.

In spite of this, the early-running habit has been very successful. Where they occur, spring salmon and early-running grilse continue to run to the headwaters to spawn. Presumably these fish behave in the way that they do because, on balance, this type of lifestyle has proved most effective over the years. The disadvantages of leaving the sea earlier than necessary must therefore be outweighed by other unknown factors. The relationship between the timing of river entry and the distance travelled before spawning is close enough to suggest that the length of the journey being made is an important factor. So perhaps run timing is an adaptation to the rigours of the journey that homing fish expect to have to undertake.

Most animals acquire access to the resources they need by competing for them, and successful, dominant individuals acquire most of what is best – to the ultimate benefit of their progeny. River catchments are not uniform and the resources available to salmon vary from location to location. Yet by homing, salmon fail to compete for what might be the best spawning locations of all. Small groups of salmon may compete locally at spawning time but, in the larger rivers, fish of the early and late runs make their journeys separately and they never even meet.

However, competition among large numbers of spawners for the best spawning places would debilitate them all. The places where salmon spawn are often suited more to the rearing of their progeny than to the comfort and safety of the spawners themselves. So spawners move into these areas late in the year, spawn quickly and move away again. If homing did not exist and if spawners crowded the most favoured spawning places, success would have to be achieved through competition. The most combative fish would win, but would pay a high price for their success by using energy from reserves already depleted by fasting. For those fish that failed to win out at first, renewed competition for inferior habitat elsewhere would be doubly debilitating. And all these arrangements would have to be made hurriedly since spawning cannot be deferred for long beyond its appointed time. So perhaps homing has arisen as a mutually beneficial arrangement that reduces the debilitation that would result from unrestrained competition among individuals or among populations. On the other hand, it is hard to imagine how potential competitors might go about reaching agreement and why they might feel compelled to stick to any arrangement later on.

The more favoured explanation for homing is that salmon from one particular place are not in competition with those from other areas because their requirements and preferences differ. Spawners may fail to compete because each group values its own special spawning places most highly among all the places that might be available. Particular places are probably sought after by different types of fish whose progeny perform better there than they do in other locations. In this case, the particular value of homing will be to ensure the perpetual matching of special types of genetically adapted fish to particular areas of streams and rivers. If adaptation to particular stream environments is an important factor in survival, the success of individuals (measured always as the success of their progeny) will usually be conditioned by how accurately they have homed.

By whatever means homing has arisen, it serves the best interests of all salmon well. Adult fish regroup in the same patterns that they formed as juveniles. So, in a stable and well-stocked river the rearing habitat used previously is evenly replenished with eggs. Because of homing, the distribution of spawners matches the proven capacity of the same locations to produce the juveniles that will go on to become returning adults themselves. As a result, eggs are deposited by successive generations in patterns that are consistent with the capacity of streams to support the greatest numbers of young fish. Overall, homing appears to ensure the greatest average success for all spawners and their progeny.

Fishing for spring salmon on the upper reaches of the River Dee.

Buchanty Spout on the River Almond comprises a set of obstacles that fish must surmount in turn. The pool between the falls appears to offer no refuge for fish that have jumped the first falls. But although the surface speed of the water is rapid, speeds are much slower nearer to the bed of the stream and at its sides. Even the most turbulent places in rivers offer respite for travelling salmon in small areas of slack water.

CHAPTER 6

The Final Run

By the middle of October, work at the Girnock Burn will have been in progress for several weeks, as juvenile salmon moving downstream are captured, counted and tagged. A few adult fish may have run into the stream already but after mid-October, spawners can be expected in greater numbers. Quite how soon the fish will begin to reach the trap, how many will arrive and when the run will cease cannot be predicted accurately. However, experience has shown that most of the adults will have entered the stream by the first week of November and that spawning will have been completed by the middle of the same month. In these respects, the Girnock Burn is typical of many spawning streams elsewhere.

Salmon usually enter the Girnock Burn when the stream is in flood. Rainfall is often carried swiftly across the catchment by weather fronts moving from beyond the mountains to the west. So periods of high rainfall are often measured only in hours and autumn floods are correspondingly short-lived. The stream's flow begins to increase about six hours after the onset of rain, as water saturates the catchment and gathers to reach the stream itself. At this point, conditions change rapidly. Flow may rise from levels of less than 0.05 to more than 20 cubic metres per second in only two or three hours. Although the stream falls back more slowly than it rises, peak flows pass quickly. So salmon waiting in the river must react rapidly to take advantage of the floodwater that will help them ascend the stream.

Earlier in the season, towards the end of the summer, salmon will move into small tributary streams, but only in response to unusually large floods. Usually these fish stay only for a brief period, leaving again quickly as the floodwater recedes. Movements like these can be seen as part of the exploratory probing that was considered in Chapter 5. In general, salmon that leave the Girnock Burn after a short stay return there later. Fish that are radio-tagged before being turned away from the fish-trap also show this pattern of activity. Radio signals from the small transmitters that these fish carry show that they return to the main river to resume their wait – downstream and within several kilometres of the stream's mouth.

Later in autumn, with the nearness of spawning, adults entering streams become fully committed to remaining there. When fish enter the Girnock Burn, they often begin arriving as darkness falls – on the whole, movement by day is not favoured. The first spates of October bring in the most receptive of the waiting fish. A week or more will elapse before the next crop of entrants is primed to respond to the next spate. As time moves on, waiting fish will respond to lesser floods. Towards mid-November, the last salmon of all may enter the Girnock Burn when stream flow is not raised at all – although even at this stage, fish still prefer to move up in flood water.

The pattern of events at the trap is mirrored in patterns of movement elsewhere. After being released above the trap, spawners continue to move upstream. As before, they usually do so by night, spending the daylight hours hidden below rafts of leaves or driftwood or in recesses under the stream banks. Again, high flows are always conducive to upstream movement and they are a prerequisite for movement early in autumn. And again, fish lower their requirements as spawning time approaches so that at full sexual maturity they will run the stream in low water and even in the hours of daylight. By the time spawning starts, salmon will be distributed throughout most of the length of the Girnock Burn. Indeed, the most intrepid fish will have travelled the whole length of the stream to spawn where it is only a metre wide.

Each year, female salmon lead the way to the trap. In many years, the first females arrive alone. In some, the first fish of both sexes are captured together, but in general, male fish tend to lag throughout the run, and at the end of it, the last fish to arrive at the trap are all males. The difference between the sexes arises because the rules that have governed the behaviour of all the fish in previous months change quickly near spawning time. As we have seen, in the run-up to spawning, many of the fish are homing. But as spawning approaches and as fish near their target locations, the single option they have pursued until now broadens into a range of competing possibilities. This is particularly the case with the males. Females act with a certain independence since they alone will determine where they will construct their redds and when they will spawn. But males must respond to these arrangements, as well as making their own accommodations with other competing males. This often leads to delay.

During the final run to the spawning grounds, a number of factors can disrupt the plans laid by salmon of either sex. In some cases, they are thwarted in their endeavours. For example, large fish homing to small streams may find it physically impossible to reach their targets, especially during periods of low flow. Fish like these fail to compete their planned journey and spawn short of their target. In other cases, fish are waylaid by unforeseen opportunities. Male fish moving purposefully upstream may be distracted by encounters with spawning females. Close encounters may be based on visual contact but information also comes in other forms. Female salmon emit chemical signals (pheromones) just before and during spawning. These pheromones are powerful sexual attractants for males, and they are effective far beyond the range of sight.

Once the first females have started to spawn, males are assailed by attractants borne by water and carried downstream. Where streams converge or where tributary streams leave rivers, signals may be carried by both bodies of water. So all male spawners except those that spawn first of all face a sequence of complex choices in deciding whether to adhere to their intended route. A measure of sexual success may be achieved in different ways but one option will usually be best. Success for males is determined by their ability to assess the value of their own options against those of other males. The effectiveness of the choices they make are determined by how well they allocate their own resources in competing for what they require in order to reproduce.

The first of the resources at the males' disposal is energy. This must be conserved as far as possible since the reserves each fish can call on are limited. The second is time. This must be managed, since each male's options reduce as it delays and as females spawn and move away. The third is their intrinsic ability to face down their competitors. They bring all these resources to bear in the quest for access to spawning females. Although they are not aware of it, their real interests are not personal. The ultimate test of each male's success at spawning is a measure of its ability to propagate the genes it carries by siring progeny. The females with which males might attempt to pair vary in their capacity to generate viable progeny and some parts of streams differ from others in the extent to which they can support the young fish. So male salmon would be expected to compete for access to particular females and they probably seek access to females spawning in particular places.

The Old Invercauld Bridge at Braemar, high on the Dee catchment. The bridge was built about 1752. Its design is credited to a Major Cauldfield of the British Army. The bridge was built as part of the road network constructed after the Jacobite Rebellion of 1745 to facilitate military control of the clan areas.

Over the years, the number of adult salmon reaching the Girnock Burn has varied widely. In years when fish have been most numerous, between 200 and 300 have been caught in the trap and released to continue their journey upstream. In other years fewer than 50 have reached the trap. However, variations in the numbers of adults spawning has surprisingly little effect on the numbers of young fish to be found in the stream later. In general, the number of young fish in the new year-class is not limited by the number of eggs laid the previous year. It is limited by the total number of living spaces available when they hatch. In years when large numbers of females spawn, more eggs are laid in the stream and more fry hatch. However, greater mortality rates soon whittle the new year-class down to its standard size. Relatively few fish are required to replenish the Girnock Burn. The eggs of about 30 females, distributed in evenly spaced redds, are sufficient to fill the stream to capacity even after mortality has taken its toll.

The River Dee near Balmoral. In 1850, Queen Victoria witnessed a display of leistering near here which she described in her book *Leaves from the Journal of Our Life in the Highlands*. The display took the form of a *battue*, using fish-spears and nets wielded by an assembly of colourful local retainers. The exercise seems to have been only a moderate success and eight fish were captured. Leistering was outlawed in 1868.

In the few years when female spawners are less numerous than this, the number of eggs deposited in the stream is too low to ensure occupancy of all the vacant living spaces. As a result, the new year-class of young fish is less numerous than usual and it produces fewer smolts in the following years. However, this effect is not as great as might be expected. At the Girnock Burn as in many streams, most juveniles become smolts at either two or three years of age. So the consequences of a single inadequate spawning year are shared between both smolt years. In addition, each new year-class interacts with the year-classes already in the stream and with those that follow. Strong year-classes following poor ones take up the space their predecessors have not been able to fill.

In 1978, no adult fish was allowed to pass beyond the Girnock trap in an experiment simulating a natural, cataclysmic failure of spawning. As a result, of course, there were no two-year-old smolts among the migrants in 1981 and 3-year-olds were absent in 1982. In 1982 however, 2-year-olds left the stream in much greater numbers than expected and the smolt run held up unexpectedly well. In the absence of the older fish, many of 1982's run had become smolts at a younger age than is usual for the Girnock Burn. Of course, these fish had been borrowed from the potential 3-year-olds of the 1983 smolt run, and as a consequence, 1983's run was also smaller than average. In the absence of a year's spawning, the deficit in smolts had been spread among the migrations of at least three years. The deficit was also spread unexpectedly uniformly. In all three years, the total number of smolts leaving the stream was still about 60 per cent of the average.

This extreme case demonstrates the robustness of salmon populations in the face of natural variation in the numbers of adult spawners. Even a total absence of spawning makes surprisingly little impact on migrant numbers, provided that the stream supports more than one age-class of young fish and provided that spawning fails only for a single year. As a result of this resilience, the number of smolts leaving the Girnock Burn each year is not normally dependent on the number of adults spawning there and it is more constant than might be expected.

Exactly when spawning takes place is determined by the females. Their choice of timing is limited: they cannot spawn before their eggs ripen fully and before the eggs are released from the membranes that bind them in the ovaries, the process known as ovulation. Salmon are unusual in lacking oviducts to deliver eggs from the ovary to the vent. Instead, the ovaries rupture at ovulation and the eggs are shed into the body cavity, remaining there for some time before being expelled from the body during spawning. But ovulated eggs lose vitality if they are retained within the body cavity for too long. So after ovulation, females are committed to spawning their eggs within a matter of days.

In spite of this constraint, females do have a measure of flexibility. They can defer spawning by delaying ovulation, so matching the time at which they must spawn to the time at which they can gain access to their chosen site. Indeed, it is quite likely that ovulation is triggered indirectly by the final burst of activity that takes females from their places of residence to their spawning locations. Levels of the sex steroid hormones fall briefly following intense swimming activity, but are restored quickly by a compensatory burst of glandular activity. This may also have the additional effect of initiating the hormonal processes that precipitate ovulation.

In the Girnock Burn, the peak spawning time is early November and most of the spawning activity is completed within about 10 days. While this pattern is typical of many other streams, the timing of spawning varies considerably, even in different places within single river catchments. In Scotland as a whole, spawning starts in late October in the major eastern rivers and finishes in mid-January in the rivers of the south-west. Within the River Dee, spawning starts in the high western catchment in late October and finishes in late December at low altitudes near the sea. The range of dates over which salmon spawn is a measure of the diversity of the habitats in which they do so. Fish maximise the chances of success for their progeny at emergence the next spring, by matching the development of their eggs with the local environment where they make their redds.

Emergence is a particularly important time in the young fishes' lives. Fry emerge onto the stream bed as the reserves of their yolk-sacs become exhausted. So those that attempt to begin to feed early in the year, while winter conditions still prevail and the food they need so pressingly is in short supply, may well die. On the other hand, those that emerge too late to claim the space required for survival may also fail. The timing of emergence is therefore crucial, and fry that emerge at the most appropriate time will succeed at the expense of those that do so too early or too late. The best date for emergence differs among rivers and streams – winter conditions prevail for longer in some locations than in others. In general, spring temperatures are reached earliest at low altitudes in the south and last of all in northern mountain streams. Adults ensure that the development of their progeny is matched with these different environments by timing their spawning appropriately. As a result, emergence occurs earlier where spring comes quickly and later where winter lingers.

Tor Heggberget of the Norwegian Institute for Nature Research has shown that salmon spawn earlier in colder rivers in Norway and later in warmer ones. On the face of it, this might seem inappropriate since early spawning might be thought to lead to early hatch in the colder rivers. But an important additional factor must be considered. The rate at which eggs develop is determined by the temperature at which they incubate. So in places where low river temperatures signal that spring is likely to come late, the development of the eggs in the redds is slowed. The outcome of this complex balance can be understood more clearly by returning to consider the River Dee. In the coldest parts of the Dee catchment, fry emerge only in June from eggs laid in late October. In the warmest locations, fry emerge in May from eggs laid only in December.

OPPOSITE   The valley of the upper Girnock Burn in early spring. The stream can be seen running through the foreground, which also includes the ruins of a long-abandoned habitation. The old pasture in the foreground around the ruins has been planted with trees. The transition from pasture to heather grouse moor is clearly visible just beyond the ruin, behind the small birch wood. In the distance are the northern corries of the mountain Lochnagar. The uppermost part of the Girnock Burn drains the nearer part of the hinterland that runs south towards the mountain.

69

In order to time their spawning to best advantage, adult fish must somehow anticipate when spring will come to the spawning location they have chosen. They must match this knowledge with an estimate of the length of time their eggs will incubate in the redd. It appears that the only information that they might use to support their decisions is an appreciation of the temperature of the water in which they will spawn. However, in temperate climates at least, temperatures at spawning time are not an accurate predictor of winter temperatures. In temperate regions like Scotland and in major rivers like the Dee, spawners are not in a position to make informed decisions about future prospects on the basis of what they know of the stream around them.

Instead, it seems more likely that the information they need is contained within them – that the timing of spawning is a genetic adaptation. Indeed, it is possible to envisage how such an adaptation might evolve. By definition, those parents that time spawning to best advantage produce the greatest numbers of progeny. Later, progeny like these will comprise the greater proportion of the next generation of spawners. We have seen before how successive generations of the same populations home to spawn in the same location. The winter environments in which eggs incubate vary greatly, even within single rivers, but, they vary least, from year to year, at the same locations. So if spawning time is heritable and if salmon home to spawn where they themselves were spawned, any advantage gained in one generation will be reinforced in later generations. Of course, local environments are not exactly the same from year to year, especially in temperate regions, and the best date for spawning will also change. Even so, the odds will still favour those fish that produce the best results, in particular places, in most years.

A pair of Girnock Burn spawners. The male, lying slightly behind the female, has a well-developed kype, giving his snout its bulbous appearance.

CHAPTER 7

Spawning

In most salmon rivers, spawning takes place throughout the catchment from just above the tide to the highest mountain streams – but always where spawning gravel has accumulated and near suitable rearing habitat for juveniles. In small streams or on shallow fords, the presence of spawning fish is often signalled first by the rhythmic disturbances they create on the surface of the water. The noise of their manouevring is surprisingly noticeable, even against the background noises that streams make themselves, and spawning fish are often heard before they are seen.

Each female constructs one or more redds, and they are often grouped in the traditional spawning areas known as fords. The term 'ford' describes exactly the areas that salmon prefer for spawning. Fording places are often located on the outflows of pools or glides, where running water shallows and the current accelerates. The stream or river bed here is often formed of loose pebbles and stones and this is the gravel in which the redds are constructed. Spawning gravel is rather coarser than the term itself might imply, comprising stones the size of a man's fist mixed with smaller ones and ranging down to rough sand. The open nature of this material and the quickening of the current over the shallow fords promotes the free flow of water through the redds. A continuous flow of well-oxygenated water through the gravel is essential for the survival of the developing eggs. Groups of pairing salmon will use the best fords intensively; other fish will choose to spawn in single pairs, making their redds in smaller areas of spawning gravel, in less typical locations.

Redds are excavated by the females shortly before spawning. Approaching the spot she has chosen, she cants to present the flat of her tail to the gravel below and flexes her body's length in short bursts of vigorous activity known as cutting. The jets of water and the vortices produced beneath her flank are sufficiently powerful to move even quite large stones. Displaced stones and gravel are moved slightly downstream during cutting and they form a pile of loose, open spoil at the tail of the resulting depression. Cutting takes place intermittently over a period of several hours and alternates with periods of rest. To rest, the female drifts away from the redd and holds behind it or to the side. Resuming her activity, she will take care to direct her efforts towards the original spot and, with time, an elongated depression several inches deep and about as long as the fish itself is created in the stream bed.

Eggs being stripped from the abdomen of a brood-fish. Salmon yield several hundred eggs for each pound of their body weight. The exact number of eggs produced by each female varies according to the fish's previous life history.

Stripping milt from a male spawner onto salmon eggs. Milt will not fertilise eggs until the sperms it contains are activated by water added to the mixture. After they have been fertilised, eggs are washed and laid down in hatchery trays where they remain during incubation. Eggs can be handled and moved about freely only for several hours after fertilisation. Thereafter, until they become eyed, any disturbance causes eggs to die.

While this is going on, the male that will eventually pair with the female is nearby, although he plays no part in preparing the redd. Sometimes, in the absence of competitors, he attends quietly. More often, however, several males compete for position, threatening and chasing each other in driving attacks. In the course of all this activity, one male somehow attains dominance over the others, taking up and continuing to defend a position beside the female. This male has the advantage over his competitors as the redd nears completion and the time for spawning approaches. At this stage, the paired fish move into position over the redd, side by side. The male displays to the female, quivering his body in spasms of activity. Quite suddenly the pair spawn, quivering and gaping together. The female emits a stream of eggs which the male immediately covers with a cloud of milt – even as the eggs are being shed.

Being slightly denser than water, the eggs fall gently into the redd and especially among the crevices and gaps opened up in the gravel below. Very few eggs are lost at this stage, because the redd's surface is lower than the stream above and water eddies within the redd because of the pile of spoil behind it. The milt cloud, caught in this eddy, will remain there for a few seconds. This is quite long enough, as fertilisation is almost instantaneous. Sperms are activated on contact with fresh water, as soon as they are released by the male. Each microscopic sperm has a motile tail that drives it through the water, although the activity is not particularly directed towards the eggs. The sperm has no source of energy for this activity other than that contained within the cell at the moment of release and this is enough to allow movement for perhaps only 20 seconds. On encountering an egg, a successful sperm blocks access for competing sperm and only one sperm fertilises each egg. Most eggs are fertilised successfully by one of the many millions of sperm released at each spawning.

Spawning streams are unstable. This gravel bank has been deposited recently by an exceptionally large flood. It will shortly be colonised by grasses and other plants, and made temporarily stable. Floods are capable of moving stones of surprising size. After temperatures have been low enough to freeze the stream bed, large stones are moved with the breaking ice. Like all sediments, spawning gravel is inherently unstable and it builds up and is carried away continually. From time to time, the distribution of spawning gravel changes markedly. In general, changes like these are temporary and streams and rivers gradually restore themselves to their original state of equilibrium.

Sexually mature parr. The lower fish is a male. Many males become mature at the parr stage before going to sea. They are sexually competent. Although recent investigations have shown that single mature parr are not as successful at spawning time as adult males, together parr cover almost half of all the eggs laid in the Girnock Burn. The upper fish is a mature female parr. This is a much rarer occurrence.

This sexually mature female parr is only the second one reported from the cold rivers of northern Europe. The fish produced 38 small eggs. Sea-going females accumulate large quantities of the pigment astaxanthin from feeding on shrimp-like crustaceans. They pass this pigment on to their eggs. Sexually mature female parr, like stream-living trout, do not contain large amounts of astaxanthin and their eggs are paler in colour.

Females shed several hundred eggs for each pound of their body weight. The exact number varies according to the sort of life the female has led. An average female however, may be assumed to shed about 5000 eggs. So even a small spawning stream in which, for example, 50 pairs of average adults spawn, will harbour about ¼ million eggs. A river receiving, say, 5000 pairs of adults will support about 25 million eggs. Each union of sperm and egg marks the beginning of life for a member of a new generation and each is a measure of the ultimate success of the parents' lives. Together, all the spawning adults comprise only a remnant of all the fish they started life with, and the outcome of their progeny's lives will be similarly ill-assured.

The final act of the female's spawning is to cover the eggs where they lie. She does this by moving gravel from the stream bed just above the open redd, using the same cutting action as she did before. Surprisingly, the eggs are little disturbed in this process, being protected among the stones in the base of the redd where they have fallen. Sometimes the female will go on to create a sequence of egg pockets, moving upstream slightly and repeating the whole process each time. When she has completed her task, the eggs are lost from view under a layer of stones, gravel and coarse sand several inches in depth. At this stage, each redd, containing one or several egg pockets, is still visible on the surface of the stream bed, showing as a clean area, free of the algal growth that discolours the undisturbed stones nearby.

The teeth of a male spawner are well developed and capable of inflicting lethal damage.

A sexually mature male parr killed by an adult spawner. The fish is lying in shallow water near an area of spawning gravel. The distinct vertical blue markings on the flank are typical of mature parr, as is the small patch of spawning fungus towards the tail. The parr's flanks have been lacerated by an adult's teeth. The parr's body has been squeezed, causing one of the mature testes to protrude through a slash in the body wall.

Closer examination of the disturbed area will show a depression at its upstream edge, where material was moved down finally to cover the last pocket of eggs. This is the completed redd and the eggs will remain here all winter, lying among the pebbles in which they have been buried. Considerable interest can be had from observing the activities of spawning salmon, although local knowledge is required to pinpoint the places that might be watched and to time any visit to best effect.

When the spawning pair are within sight, the preliminary jousting of the males, the cutting of the redd, and perhaps even spawning itself may be witnessed. Indeed, these activities are sometimes carried out in water of such shallowness that the backs of the spawners are exposed from time to time. But the low angle of the winter sun limits the bankside observer's ability to see beyond the surface of the water and reflection obscures most of the detail of what might be seen. A clearer view may be obtained from a vantage point high above the spawning fords, but then the finer details of spawning are always obscured by distance and by the broken surface of the water. A different type of approach is necessary to find out what exactly is going on.

A female salmon cutting her redd. Lying on her side, the female uses a vigorous swimming motion to produce currents below her flank that displace stones and gravel downstream. After several hours she will spawn her eggs in the resulting depression. The female covers her eggs by cutting again just upstream from where the eggs lie. This redd had been completed by the following day.

In his authoritative book, J.W. Jones[9] devoted considerable space to describing his observations of salmon as they spawned in large glass-sided tanks built into the bank of a tributary of the Welsh Dee. Conditions in tanks are always unnatural and the circumstances in which fish are brought together are contrived, but using tanks to observe fish was the best approach that was available at that time and Jones was able to document many aspects of spawning that had not been described before. In more recent years, unrestrained fish in natural streams have been observed using underwater television cameras. This approach has also produced new insights. Television pictures have revealed many aspects of the social arrangements of fish spawning naturally that cannot be observed directly from the stream bank or in tanks.

9. J.W. Jones. *The Salmon*, Collins, London, 1959.

Using television, courting behaviour, competition, cutting and spawning can all be viewed in some detail. It becomes clear immediately that many more fish are present during spawning than the single adult pair that dominates the scene. The adults are commonly outnumbered by trout and salmon parr. Sometimes 30 or 40 parr can be seen in and around the redd. Most of the salmon parr can be identified as sexually mature males by their distinct coloration and presumably they attend spawning with a sense of expectation. In general, adult salmon ignore the parr around them but occasionally they will engage in a brief attack. Indeed, some mature parr pay for their ardour with their lives; their crushed and bitten bodies are occasionally found on the streambed where spawning has taken place.

It has been known for many years that male parr become sexually mature and that their milt is capable of fertilising eggs. J.W. Jones was aware that male parr also participate in natural spawning. He made the study of their behaviour an important component of the work he performed in his observation tanks. Jones concluded that, although mature parr were fully capable of producing progeny, their role as parents was rather limited. On their own, the small, inconspicuous parr were not capable of stimulating the full repertoire of sexual behaviour in females. Females performed properly only when sea-run, adult males were there to court them and they would not spawn in the presence of parr alone. On the basis of what he saw, Jones concluded that mature male parr represented a form of insurance against failure by the large adult males to carry out their role in reproduction to its proper conclusion. Recent work has shown that Jones was not correct on this point. Mature parr operate successfully on the redds – not in outright competition with large males but by subverting their privileges.

Television pictures give some idea of how this may occur. As spawning takes place the female and the adult male hold position side by side, a few inches above the base of the redd depression that the female has cut in the stream bed. The parr are grouped loosely around and within this area, deep within the roughness of the gravel. Those parr lying in the redd base itself, close to the female's vent, appear to be particularly well placed to fertilise the female's eggs. But beyond this, observation is not capable of providing the sort of information that is required to understand what actually takes place. Spawning starts suddenly. The stream of eggs emitted by the females is enveloped immediately in a diffuse cloud of milt. The capacity of the spawning adult male to produce milt greatly exceeds that of all the male parr to do so. The greater part of the milt cloud can probably be attributed to the adult male alone. On the other hand, the advantage of greater proximity to the female's eggs may offset the parrs' lack of sexual capacity.

Only recently has it become possible to examine the parrs' role in spawning with any rigour, using powerful new genetic techniques. It has been shown that, as a group, mature parr are rather successful in siring progeny, and they cover very many of the females' eggs. This discovery, and others like it, have been made possible by the recent development of the so-called single-locus genetic probes by John Taggart of Queen's University in Belfast and Diogo Tomaz of the University of Leicester. These probes are a development of the DNA 'fingerprinting' techniques that are familiar to most people through newspaper reports of their use in forensic science. The new DNA probes are simpler and more powerful than previous techniques, and can be used as heritable genetic tags, passed from parents to their progeny, linking the old and the new generations. Genetic tags have made it possible to perform research now that could not be contemplated before.

The probes are only now beginning to be used to unlock the secrets of the lives of salmon, but when their power is more widely understood, their development will come to be recognised as one of the most important technical advances of recent years. The extent of the power they offer has already been glimpsed in work carried out at the Girnock Burn. The aim of these studies has been to find out how particular individuals contribute to the generation of each new year class.

Finding redds again, in spring. When the redds are constructed in autumn, photography is used to record this position against fixed landmarks on the stream's bank and on its bed. A helper points out the location with a staff. After the winter, the redds are no longer visible on the stream bed, but the photographic record is used to pinpoint the redd's position.

Sampling eggs in spring from a redd made in autumn. The top of the egg pocket lies just below the surface of the stream bed. A draw hoe is used with care to remove surface gravel and when eggs are exposed they are gathered in a net.

The new DNA probes detect genetic differences among fish. Each parent contributes half of its own genetic material to each of its progeny. In the same way, the genetic material of every one of their progeny is derived equally from each of the parents. The genetic make-ups of parents and progeny are therefore closely linked. Using the probes to 'fingerprint' the parents' genetic make-ups, it is possible to predict the genetic fingerprints of their progeny. In the Girnock experiments, John Taggart has worked back the other way, from progeny to parents. The genetic fingerprints of embryos taken from each redd were used to deduce which female had spawned there and with which adult male she had paired.

To carry out these studies, the fish-trap on the Girnock Burn was used to intercept all the adults ascending the stream to spawn. Small samples of fin tissue were obtained from each adult allowed to ascend the stream beyond the trap. These samples were used to type the genetic make-up of each of the adults – and therefore of each of the potential adult spawners in the stream. Just after spawning had taken place, the stream bed was surveyed to find the redds made by the females. At this stage, the eggs within the redds did not contain sufficient DNA for fingerprinting. So all the places in which females had spawned, or where it was thought they might have spawned, were marked for later reference. This was done by taking photographs of each redd's location among fixed reference points in the stream and on its banks. The eggs were allowed to develop naturally in the gravel over the winter months. In March the redds were relocated. By this time, the embryos within the eggs had developed sufficiently to be recognisable as small fish and each egg contained more than enough DNA for genetic typing. Each redd was opened up by gently removing stones and gravel until the topmost of the eggs were exposed. A small number of eggs was removed, and the rest covered up again with gravel and left to continue incubation in the normal way. The embryos contained within the sampled eggs were genetically fingerprinted in the same way as the adults had been.

In 1991, 87 salmon entered the Girnock Burn and were allowed to ascend beyond the fish-trap to spawn in the stream above. Thirty-one of the fish were males and 56 were females. Seventy-two potential redds were located shortly after spawning had taken place. Five months later, samples of eggs were obtained from 57 of these locations but not from the other 15. On the face of it, this looked like a fairly simple situation where the number of true redds was very nearly equivalent to the number of females and where a number of false starts had been included in the count. In fact, the results of our experiment gave the lie to this picture of simplicity. And from here on, matters become complex.

First, it was discovered that of the 57 redds from which eggs were obtained, 11 contained the progeny of more than a single female. Some of the females had cut their redds and spawned their eggs in places that had been used earlier by other females. This phenomenon is known as over-cutting. The progeny of only 34 of the 56 females were found in all the redds discovered. The progeny of the other 22 were not located. Three of the females whose progeny were missing were found killed by otters, and it is possible that they met their end before they spawned. Another seven of the females whose progeny were missing were not seen again after being passed beyond the fish-trap. Otters sometimes conceal fish they have killed and foxes sometimes carry carcasses left by otters away from the vicinity of the stream. So the missing fish may also have been killed before spawning, without this being noticed. On the other hand, another 10 females whose progeny were also not discovered were recaptured at the fish trap as kelts, moving downstream shortly after they had spawned. So either the places that had contained these fishes' eggs in autumn no longer contained them in spring, or their progeny had been hidden in over-cut redds.

In any case, by March, 68 groups of eggs could be identified, laid by 34 females in 57 locations. Three females had made four redds each, three had made three each and 11 had made two. The remaining females had made only one each. Larger females tended to make more redds than smaller fish, typically spacing them out over a restricted area of stream less than 100m long. Interestingly, when single females made several redds they often paired with different adult males to do so. For example, the fish designated Female 24 made four redds. To do this she paired with a different adult male on each occasion – Males 72, 28, 15 and 63. Female 27 made four redds. She also paired with Male 72 to make three of her redds and with Male 44 to make the other. Female 37 made three of her four redds with the same Male 44 and the other with another male that could not be identified. It appears, therefore, that constancy is not widely observed among pairing salmon.

Male 72 and Male 44 have figured prominently so far, each pairing with two of the females chosen as examples. In fact, Male 72 paired at a total of six redds with three different females and Male 44 paired at five redds, also with three different females. Paternity could not be established with certainty for 19 of the 68 groups of eggs located in the stream. But paternity among all the remaining 49 could be attributed to only 18 of the 31 adult males present in the stream. Two males (including Male 72) paired at six redds, one (Male 44) at five, two others at four redds, two at three and seven at two. Only four males paired at a single redd. A disproportionate number of all the pairings that took place were therefore covered by only a few of all the adult males that were present. The smaller adult males appeared to lose out to larger ones in competing for access to females.

Salmon eggs lying within the confines of the redd, where they have been exposed by a researcher's digging. The range of sizes in spawning gravel can be judged by the size of the eggs – they are about 5mm in diameter. Spawning gravel is a porous mixture of coarse sands, large pebbles and small stones. Free flow of water through the gravel is essential for the eggs' survival.

In most of the redds, some of the progeny could not be attributed to the adult male that had covered most of the group, and they were not the progeny of any of the other adult males that had entered the stream. Instead, they had been fathered by resident small male parr. In general, individual parr made small contributions to paternity and the contributions of several of these sneakers could be recognised in the same redd. It is not known whether a large proportion of all the mature parr in the stream succeed in sneaking; nor is it known precisely how successful individual sneakers are. But taken together these small contributions add up and, as a group, parr show themselves to be very successful indeed. On average, 40 per cent of the progeny in redds were sired by small sneakers and the greatest value for a single redd was 60 per cent.

Ultimately, reproduction is the main focus of all fishes' lives and it must be taken to be the main reason for the parrs' presence near the redd. But this is not the whole story. Parr eat substantial numbers of eggs. In fact, these small fish sometimes eat so many eggs that characteristic round protuberances appear on their belly surface, caused by the tight mass of eggs packed into the stomach. Dissection shows that, at spawning time, parr between about 100 and 120mm in length may contain a dozen or so eggs and this may be only one of several similar meals. Eggs are evidently highly palatable and parr only 70mm long strain to swallow eggs 4 or 5mm in diameter. Whether the parr that fertilise eggs eat them too or whether parr eat eggs that they have fertilised themselves is not known.

For many parr the effects of their opportunism are long-lasting. The fat content of a dozen salmon eggs is approximately equivalent to the entire fat reserves of a parr's body. So the potential nutritive value of the eggs they consume is substantial. Indeed, parr can be shown to digest and assimilate at least some of the fats and oils they consume by eating eggs. Fats are made up of a mixture of different molecules that are known collectively as fatty acids. Particular fatty acids can be separated and identified in the laboratory. The fat that fish store during feeding at sea differs in its fatty acid composition from fat accumulated by feeding in fresh water. The fats in eggs are derived from the body fats of adult females. This means that the fats in eggs are of the marine type, since the female's body fat is laid down during marine feeding. When parr eat eggs at spawning time, the composition of their body fat changes to become more like marine fat. This change persists over the winter and until spring, when the resumption of feeding in fresh water finally restores the fat to its normal fresh-water type.

At this point, it is worth recalling that trout are also present among the parr attending spawning. Trout scavenge around the redds and, like salmon parr, they eat salmon eggs. It might be thought likely that the prospect of a free meal would be the trouts' sole reason for being present on the redd. Surprisingly, however, this is not the whole story. Trout sometimes participate in the spawning of salmon, fertilising their eggs to produce hybrid progeny. Trout and salmon differ genetically and hybrids have a genetic make-up that is intermediate between that of pure salmon and pure trout. Such hybrids are rather uncommon in nature; but by

A salmon-trout hybrid. Fish like these are produced when salmon and trout spawn together. The appearance of hybrids is intermediate between trout and salmon. In the photograph, the long upper jaw and the thick 'wrist' are trout-like features in a fish that otherwise looks like a salmon. Hybrid fish can be identified with certainty only in the laboratory. Genetic tests show that half the genes that hybrids contain are those of salmon and half are those of trout. Laboratory tests can also reveal the species of the mother and father that paired to produce the hybrid. Most of the hybrids that have been identified in Scotland have proved to be the progeny of female salmon. Interestingly, the situation is reversed in North America – most hybrids there are the progeny of female trout. Hybrid fish appear to be quite rare in nature and most have been discovered among young fish sampled from streams. Only ten or so proven hybrids have been found among adult fish. The unofficial record for a rod-caught hybrid (or indeed, any hybrid) stands at 7lb (3.2kg).

chance, one of the families spawned during the experiment at the Girnock Burn in 1991 was a hybrid family. As we saw before, Female 27 spawned with Male 72 on three occasions. Sneakers had been active as all three redds were made. In two of the redds sneaking was by two or three salmon parr, as is normal. In the third, however, sneaking had been by a male trout and it had covered more than half of the eggs sampled. This trout could not be identified as one of the few large trout that had ascended the Girnock Burn near spawning time. It was a small resident trout that had sneaked paternity in the same way as the salmon parr.

In general, hybrids are rare among juvenile salmonids and among catches of adults. Pairings between trout and salmon must be presumed to be similarly infrequent. Indeed, in spite of their living and breeding in close proximity, trout and salmon have managed to retain their separate species identities. Some hybrids, at least, are sterile 'mules', and these fish are unable to mix the species further by passing on their salmon genes to trout or their trout genes to salmon. However, hybrids are so uncommon that some other barrier must limit the initial crossing between trout and salmon. Interestingly, whatever this barrier is, it appears to be lowered where salmon that have escaped from fish farms spawn. For some unknown reason, when escaped salmon spawn in rivers they produce more hybrid progeny than wild fish do. The progeny of escaped females are about ten times more likely to be sired by trout than those of wild fish and about one in ten of the progeny of escaped females is a hybrid.

CHAPTER 8

The Genetics of Salmon

As we have seen, every phase of the life of salmon is variable. A bewildering array of lifestyles can be constructed by piecing together all the forms of every phase. Yet in some respects groups of salmon from the same rivers or even from the same places in single rivers, are often rather similar. Some rivers are noted for the size of their fish, some for a profusion of grilse, some are noted for numbers of spring-running salmon and others for the strength of their autumn runs. Within river catchments, too, tributaries differ. Particular tributaries often produce smolts that are characteristically younger or older than the river's average. Likewise, some tributaries produce smolts that are larger or smaller than average for their age. Different tributaries receive different types of adults at spawning time. Some parts of rivers receive runs that are made up mostly of grilse, while other parts receive runs of larger 2SW salmon. All these differences and all the similarities are entirely attributable to one or both of only two effects: the fishes' genetic make-up and the environment in which they live.

Each salmon's life is shaped by every aspect of the social and physical environment in which it lives. For example, fish tend to grow more slowly when they lead their lives in a social environment that is crowded by other fish competing for the same food. But the availability of the food that will support the growth of fish is determined in part by temperature – an aspect of the physical environment. In addition, the rate at which fish will find it intrinsically possible to grow, even in the presence of unlimited food, is determined by the effect of temperature on their body processes. Cold tends to slow these down.

As a result of the interplay of effects like these, groups of young salmon growing at colder locations are smaller than groups growing in warmer places. Fish from each group are more similar to each other than to members of other groups. Growth affects many other aspects of fishes' lives. To some extent, the growth rate of juveniles determines their performance later on. So differences established in groups of young salmon may still be apparent after the fish have dispersed to live together in the sea. Indeed, differences may still exist even after adults part again to return to their own rivers.

The environment is a powerful shaping tool but the basic form of each fish's life is defined by the nature of the starting material formed by its genes. Some genes code specifically for the proteins that are central to all life's processes. The action of these is regulated by yet other genes. Many genes take different forms that vary in their effects and the outcome of the processes they support is sometimes noticeably different. As a matter of fact, like all other animals, each individual salmon is genetically unique. On the other hand, all the genes combine to produce individuals that are similar enough to be recognised as salmon and grouped together as a single species. Beyond this, salmon are also grouped in smaller units. Local populations can be shown to exist by considering the genetic make-up of individuals living in different places.

Like all animals, salmon contain many genes. The exact number is not known but each fish contains somewhere between 50,000 and 100,000 genes. (At this point, it becomes necessary to introduce the only really technical term to be found in the whole of this book. Even this is a matter for regret, but the word in question has no counterpart in everyday language, and any attempt to avoid using it by misusing other more familiar terms will lead us slowly into a web of contradictions and misunderstanding. The word in question is 'allele'.) Each gene comprises two parts, known as alleles, that function separately and equally as components of the

Fishing the Tay, Scotland's largest river. The Tay is more than 160km long and it drains a catchment extending to 500sq km.

In many places, rivers and their bank-sides are among the wildest places and the most natural habitats that remain. Unspoiled rivers support a diverse range of wildlife. Some anglers regard their quarry species as being of overriding importance. In truth, however, game fish form only a small part of a large complex web of interdependent species that is best enjoyed as a whole.

gene unit. Each fish inherits one allele for every gene from its mother and one from its father. It carries this complement unchanged throughout its life. In every fish, all the cells of the body contain all the genes and (with the special exceptions of sperm or egg cells) both alleles for every gene. When fish become sexually mature they donate only one allele for every gene – at random – to every egg or sperm they produce. When an egg and a sperm combine at fertilisation, the single alleles they contain combine to form the new pairs that constitute the new progeny's genes. Genes are split and recombined like this each time spawning takes place.

Unfortunately, it is technically impossible to examine most of the genes that fish possess, although a great deal of useful information has been gathered on the few that we can. In particular, a number of genes that code for the proteins known as enzymes have been studied intensively. Each of the paired alleles that constitute these genes causes amino acids to link up precisely into chains. These chains form the basic structure of the particular enzyme the gene codes for. Enzymes are crucially important substances that drive the biochemical reactions on which life depends.

Some genes are variable; they take different forms and they occur as paired combinations of common and variant alleles. In the simplest case, we can consider two different forms of an allele, A and B. In individual fish, three different combinations of paired alleles are possible – A-A, A-B and B-B. Each allele functions independently and the forms of the enzyme produced by A and B alleles differ slightly. In A-A or B-B fish both alleles are identical and each of these fish contains only a single enzyme of the form corresponding to the A or B allele. In A-B fish the paired alleles produce both forms of the enzyme. The forms of the enzyme can be distinguished using the technique known as electrophoresis and the identity of the allele pairings present in individual fish can be determined. Using this information, the frequency of the different alleles in fish from single populations can be estimated by counting up the contributions made by individuals.

Although the enzymes produced by the A and B alleles differ slightly, they act in the same way. Slight differences in the enzyme produced by one variable allele, among all the many genes a fish possesses, would not be expected to produce important changes in the fish's overall performance. It is usually assumed therefore that the different allele pairings have no particular effect on the lives of the salmon in which they occur. This assumption means that the different alleles can be used as passive or 'neutral' markers to follow the movement of genetic material among populations. Information compiled for different genes and their alleles can be combined to produce a genetic picture that can be used to define and describe salmon populations.

Thirty or 40 enzyme genes have been examined routinely in salmon sampled from streams and rivers across northern and western Europe and eastern America. Most of these genes are made up of pairs of identical alleles. The more informative genes are those in which the alleles regularly take more than a single form. Most of our information on the genetics of salmon populations is based on only four or five genes of this type.

The same alleles tend to be present in all salmon populations. However, distinct differences exist in the frequencies with which they occur. Populations separated by the greatest distances differ most. The populations of the eastern and western Atlantic coasts differ most of all. In fact the difference is so great that the Atlantic salmon of North America might be considered quite distinct from those of Europe. Smaller differences exist among populations within Europe and Canada and among populations within countries like Scotland. Even on the finest scale, small but real genetic differences exist among the tributary populations of some major rivers.

Because this genetic variation is assumed to be neutral, the differences between populations are attributed to the effects of random processes. For instance, the frequencies of variant alleles in populations tend to differ between successive generations solely as a matter of chance. These minor differences accumulate with time, causing allele frequencies to drift randomly from their original values, and populations diverge gradually as a result. In contrast, the process known as bottle-necking takes place suddenly, after a population has been reduced to small numbers and squeezed through a genetic constriction at some stage in its history. Again, it is likely that allele frequencies in the few remaining fish will differ from those in the original population by chance alone. Any differences will persist as the population expands its numbers once again, when the bottle-neck has been passed. Founder effects are similar. They occur when a new population is founded by a small number of fish that have strayed from elsewhere. Under these circumstances, it is quite likely, again by chance, that the new population will differ from the old one. Changes produced by all these effects are permanently incorporated into populations because, as we have seen, most salmon home with surprising accuracy before they spawn.

A female goosander foraging in winter. Goosanders were previously birds of the Scandinavian forests and rivers but the species has extended the limits of its range southwards over the last century. Goosanders' eyes are positioned on the front of the face, giving the stereoscopic vision that lets the birds hunt fish by sight. Young salmon and trout form a portion of the diet. In Britain, goosanders are a protected species and their control is strictly regulated.

A group of goosanders that have assembled to rest in a quiet backwater between periods of feeding. Excursions are made upstream, commonly on the wing. Feeding birds drift back slowly on the river's flow, diving to fish runs and pools as they pass. The passage of each bird into the resting area is associated with much social behaviour among those birds that are already there.

On the other hand, straying must sometimes occur or new populations would not be established at all. In fact, it has been suggested that straying may prove more worthwhile than homing for some fish, allowing them to spawn in places that have not contained salmon before. As a general rule, the progeny of strayers like these would be expected to prove unusually successful because of the absence of competing families. Straying is difficult to examine because it is not possible to anticipate where strayed fish will turn up. Sometimes tagged fish are located in rivers far from their original source, usually by anglers, and these fish are often assumed to be strayers. However, many fish like these may rectify their mistakes before spawning. Only at spawning do strayers contribute their alleles to the recipient population and this is the real test of straying.

Of course, all salmon populations were originally founded by strayers. More particularly, many of the rivers which support salmon now were covered previously by the ice-sheets of the last glaciation. As the ice receded, most of the new rivers would have been devoid of salmon. Present-day populations were founded by strayers from other rivers that had not been sterilised by the ice. Straying probably still occurs today in much the same way. Straying will foster the exchange of alleles, tending to make their frequencies uniform everywhere. Straying fish will tend to break down genetic differences among populations. But founder effects and the effects of genetic drift and bottle-necking can still be measured today, so where straying does occur, it does not occur frequently enough to counterbalance the results of these effects. The forces isolating salmon populations are therefore greater than those bringing them together.

It is possible to estimate the extent of straying among populations by comparing the frequencies of alleles at the variable genes. For example, the Rivers Shin, Oykel and Carron, in the Kyle of Sutherland catchment in northern Scotland, share a common estuary. The genetic make-up of each of the rivers' salmon populations has been examined and the differences between the rivers suggest the effective straying of only about 20 individuals to each river in every generation. The number of fish spawning in each of the rivers is not known but they must be counted in thousands. So the estimated number of effective strayers is very small in relation to the size of the populations. In fact, the number is so small that it may stretch credulity. However, to be considered an *effective* strayer, the straying fish's progeny must survive as well as the river's native fish. Moreover, the progeny must return to spawn at the same rate as native fish, and so on through the generations. In other words, to become an effective strayer the straying fish must contribute its alleles fully and permanently to the recipient population.

Because of homing, new alleles tend to be retained in the population in which they arise rather than being shared with other populations. Many new alleles are probably neutral in their effects, as we have seen. On the other hand some will alter the performance of the fish that carry them. Ultimately, the fate of these alleles is determined by the performance of the fish. If a new allele debilitates the fish that carry it, they will not survive to spawn and the alleles will be eliminated. But if the new alleles enhance performance, their frequency will increase over the generations and the population concerned will diverge from others. Often, alleles will prove advantageous only in particular localities and, in time, the populations living in these places will come to differ from those living elsewhere.

As it happens, examining the supposedly neutral genes which code for the enzymes referred to previously has proved useful in understanding genetic adaptation. In particular, the variable gene known as MEP-2 appears not to be neutral in its effects, in spite of the usual assumption to the contrary. Differences in performance are associated with the different forms of the gene.

The MEP-2 gene codes for an enzyme that controls one of the many biochemical reactions which are important in the metabolism of salmon. Two different MEP-2 alleles occur and they are designated the 100 and 125 forms. Like the A and B alleles we considered earlier, the paired MEP-2 alleles occur in individual fish randomly, in any of three combinations – 100-100, 100-125, or 125-125. The frequencies of the two alleles vary markedly in different populations in a way that appears to correspond with spring or summer temperatures. The 100 allele predominates in southern populations while the 125 form does so at northern latitudes. Frequencies change gradually between the two extremes in the intermediate part of the salmon's range. On a finer scale, the frequencies of the MEP-2 alleles in salmon populations in different parts of the same river differ in a similar way. In the River Dee and in the Kyle of Sutherland rivers for example, the 125 allele is more common at higher altitudes where streams are colder and the 100 allele is more common in warmer lowland populations. The distribution of the alleles suggests that natural selection favours the 125 allele in cold locations and the 100 allele in warm ones.

The frequencies of the MEP-2 alleles in the Kyle of Sutherland rivers are worth considering further. The River Shin was dammed in 1957 to increase the natural capacity of Loch Shin. The dam has a capacity of 230 million cubic metres and it is now effectively the river's source through the release of compensation flow. It is probable that the construction of the dam altered environmental temperatures in the river below it, particularly in spring and early summer when stored winter water is discharged. Before the dam was built, the River Shin was fed by water spilling from the surface of the natural Loch Shin. This surface water was probably warmer than water at deeper levels because of stratification. Today, however, the dam discharges from the depth of between 5 and 10m and the river is probably cooler now than it was in the past. Interestingly, the frequencies of the MEP-2 alleles in the salmon population below the dam are consistent with present-day temperatures. This suggests that the genetic make-up of Shin salmon has changed over the last 30 or 40 years to match their new environment.

The obvious conclusion to be drawn from these findings is that fish bearing the alternative MEP-2 alleles (or the different paired allele combinations) experience different measures of success in different locations. It is difficult to measure success itself but it is possible to show that the performance of individuals possessing each of the three allele combinations differs. At the Girnock Burn and also in the River Tay, fish bearing the 100-125 combination are most likely to be grilse. Among juvenile fish in the Girnock Burn, growth rate differs among the three allele combinations, although the best growth is not shown consistently by any one type. This may explain why both MEP-2 alleles and all three allele combinations continue to occur in most salmon populations. The advantages of carrying either allele may not be outright, except perhaps in the extreme environments at the limits of the salmon's range.

All of the most complex body processes, like growth and sexual maturity, are controlled by assemblages of genes acting in concert. It might be thought strange that variations of the single MEP-2 gene among the many might exert such easily measured effects on two such obvious performance traits. But it is possible that the MEP-2 gene appears important only by proxy. Rather than acting on its own, the MEP-2 gene may act as a marker for differences in larger genetic units composed of other, more important, genes.

Within the last two decades, advances in technique have made it possible for fisheries scientists to investigate the lives of salmon in ways that were unguessed at by their predecessors. As time passes, our account will come to be seen as an incomplete and inadequate snapshot of how matters really are. Looking forward, it is clear that much remains to be discovered by continuing to employ the techniques that are available now. Moreover, the pace of technical development has been so rapid over the last decade, especially in the field of medical genetics, that it seems very likely that even more power will become available in the near future. In time, these new medical techniques will come to be applied to other fields, including fisheries genetics.

To date however, only a tiny fraction of all the genes which exist in salmon have been examined. Even then, only a small number of representative populations have been documented. Against all the odds, the information gained has proved interesting and useful too. Above all, genetic studies demonstrate that salmon populations have a life of their own that is even more complex than the separate lives of their members.

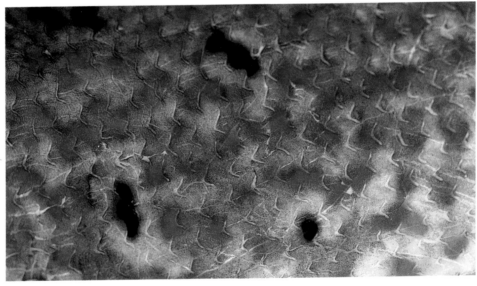

The skin of a male salmon in autumn, in full spawning livery. The dark markings are due to the pigment melanin. The red-orange pigment astaxanthin is accumulated during feeding in the sea. Towards spawning time, astaxanthin is moved from the muscles to the skin, imparting a red or an orange colour depending on the exact chemical form the pigment takes. This male had entered the river in the spring, six or seven months previously. Salmon do not feed in fresh water and, with time, wasting of the body results. Wasting has caused much of the material of this fish's scales to be resorbed. Almost none of the external part of the scales remains and the skin is uniformly smooth. The scales' positions are indicated by the ranks of pale chevrons marking the edge of the pocket of skin in which each scale is located.

Angling is a recreation that is best started young. In his collection of essays *Rod and Line*, Arthur Ransome considered the case of an acquaintance 'not in his first youth, who had wasted the flower of his life on business and golf and gardening and motoring and marriage, and had in this way postponed his initiation far too long'.

CHAPTER 9

The Structure of Populations

Separate genetic populations of salmon exist because enough adults home with sufficient precision to keep the breeding groups to which they belong separate. Populations can only be examined where the breeding groups are sufficiently separate to make the differences between them detectable. In seeking to make the genetic measurements necessary to define populations, it must be decided at which point to break into the repeating cycle of the generations. Two particular stages of the salmon's life, when populations are most sharply focussed, offer the best chance of finding any structuring that may exist: after adults have dispersed to the sea and reassembled for spawning, and before dispersal, while their progeny remain near to the places where they emerged from the gravel. In the other stages of life, after fish smolt and before they return to spawn, the populations to which they belong are widely dispersed and partly or completely mixed.

Catching and sampling large numbers of adult salmon in the brief time for which they come together for spawning is not usually practicable. Juveniles can be sampled much more readily because they are accessible for a considerable period of time before dispersing to the sea. Indeed, for at least a year after they hatch, most of the young fish in any year-class remain relatively close to the places where they began life. For the most part, scientists have chosen the easier option and research work has concentrated on examining the structure and organisation of juvenile populations. In any case, because our concern here is with genetics, we can regard each year-class of young fish as being very closely linked indeed with the group of adults that spawned it. Studying the genetics of juvenile populations is a convenient and powerful way of finding out most of what we need to know about population structure.

As we have seen, genetic differences can be identified among groups of juveniles taken from different places, and population structure among and even within rivers can begin to be discerned. Despite numerous studies, however, good definition and fine detail remain elusive. Populations of salmon cannot be described with geographical precision, something which should come as no surprise. The life of a population is a continuous set of the life cycles of its members. The condition of juvenile populations reflects the behaviour of their predecessors and especially of their own parents. And we have seen how complex the biology of returning fish can be.

Even so, it is perhaps unfortunate that population biology lacks the simplicity that would make it so much easier to explain. Some of the most important concepts are subtle, and none of the rules is hard and fast. Because of this, scientists resort to describing populations in terms of what is generally found to be true – in terms of likelihoods and probabilities. So, for the lay reader, understanding population biology is a challenge. It is fashionable in some circles to profess a distrust of these sorts of complexities and an affection for simplicity, but in truth the difficulties of coming to terms with population biology lessens the significance of its message for fisheries management not one jot.

In the past, a failure to master the intricacies of genetics has meant that the concept of the population has been given a spurious authority. In a novel version of the Chinese whisper, the biologists' message has not been distorted; instead, it has been stripped of its complexity and stated more boldly than the facts warrant. In this way, many rivermen appear to feel that salmon populations ought to be completely distinct from one another and that the members of different populations ought to be clearly distinguishable. However, considered from the point of view of the protein genes (the only really solid information that we have), rigid genetic distinctions like these do not exist.

It is possible, of course, that the genetic techniques available to researchers today are not good enough for the tasks demanded of them. Even the most modern genetic techniques may not be sufficiently powerful to detect distinctions among populations that really do exist. On balance, however, it is much more likely that salmon populations are not sealed, individually wrapped packages and that leakage among then is commonplace. Thus, the same genes are almost always to be found in different populations. As a general rule, single populations cannot be shown to contain special genetic material that distinguishes their members from the members of other populations. Individual populations lack well-defined centres or clear-cut boundaries and their shape and composition vary from time to time. All this fluidity makes salmon populations difficult to describe and therefore difficult to manage. But the same fluidity lends populations a measure of flexibility and resilience, properties of crucial importance that permit them to adjust their nature constantly to match changing conditions.

We have seen that many adult salmon return to the Girnock Burn with apparent facility. And although the necessary information is lacking, there is no reason to believe that some Girnock fish do not continue to home with even greater precision once they pass beyond the fish-trap. On the other hand, salmon cannot be expected to be capable of redd-to-redd precision. Most fry move away from the immediate vicinity of the redds from which they emerge to live their juvenile lives some short distance away. The information on which the homing of adults depends is biased towards the locations where they live as parr. So adults homing to the very best of their ability will not return precisely to the places where they first started life. As a result, the pattern of distribution of adults at spawning time will always be more diffuse than it had been when they emerged from the redds to start their lives.

Fishing a jumper-net. The netsman has waited until the falling tide has made the head of the net accessible. He is using a hand-net to capture fish trapped in the fish court. The fish court is separated from the outer chambers of the net by a narrow door set in the panel of netting that seals the court. Nets like these are fished with the tides, twice each day.

On occasion, the limits of the spawners' distribution are very diffuse indeed. Errors or opportunism sometimes take salmon into rivers far from their own origins. As we saw in Chapter 6, it can often be supposed that these are temporary mistakes that are rectified before spawning time and before strayers have the opportunity to make the only permanent mark that they can, contributing their genes to their adopted population. In some cases, however, it seems quite unreasonable to suppose that the wanderings observed might be cut short.

For example, Jim Kerr, the Superintendent of the Don District Salmon Fishery Board, gathered up spawning stock in October 1992 to fill the hatchery on upper Donside. As the fish were handled it was noticed that two of the 70 salmon collected were without adipose fins. This is the mark used by biologists everywhere to indicate that fish bear microtags. Microtags are tiny slips of stainless steel wire about 1mm long that are inserted into the nasal cartilage just below the skin of the fish's snout. They are magnetised so that they can be detected in living fish. In addition, each tag bears a unique notched code along its edge that can be read to discover where the fish was tagged. Both of the microtagged fish captured on the Don had strayed there from some distance away. The less travelled fish had been tagged as a smolt two years earlier as it left the Girnock Burn. The Girnock Burn and the Don hatchery are separated, as the crow flies, by only 15km of mountain. But, as the fish swims, they are separated by 160km of river and by the 3km of sea that separate the Dee and Don estuaries. The second tagged fish had been released in an ocean-ranching project based at Kollafjord in south-east Iceland, almost 1600km to the north.

Both these fish were captured late in the year and close to spawning. It seems very likely that, in the natural course of events, both would have attempted to spawn and to leave their genes somewhere in the upper reaches of the River Don. The Icelandic fish was probably a rare and exceptional case – indeed, it had been reared in captivity for part of its life and its wanderings may have been occasioned in some way by this experience. The case of the Dee fish was probably less rare – it is easy to imagine that fish might stray between adjacent rivers quite often. Nevertheless, all the evidence suggests that even if straying among rivers is quite frequent, spawners do not contribute their genes freely to their adopted populations. And obviously, the effect of past straying has been insufficient to eradicate the population structuring that can be seen today.

In the particular case of salmon, some of the factors that make homing more straightforward also tend to make long-distance straying less likely. The final part of each adult's return route is marked by a series of abrupt discontinuities, as well marked as motorway intersections, where decisive action is required. Where rivers meet the sea, for example, no intermediate course is possible. As each river is passed, salmon can choose only to enter it or to continue onwards. In the same way, fish homing to particular tributary streams must make similar decisions each time they pass any other tributary on their journey upstream.

In addition, the final part of the salmon's return track is one-dimensional. Migratory species that move on land or in the air can deviate to right or to left, but these sorts of errors are not possible for salmon once they leave the sea. The river's width defines the salmon's only route upstream as tightly as a motorway leads traffic onwards. In these circumstances, each turn correctly made makes final homing more likely. Equally, successful completion of each segment of the intended homeward journey limits any scope for straying later on.

In any journey, haste or delay may lead to confusion and errors. In salmon, lack of time may lead to straying among late entrants to rivers or among fish that are

Bringing in the catch. Salmon netting in all its forms is an old and honourable way of making a hard living. Salmon netting has taken place in one form or another for centuries. Recent increases in the production of farmed salmon have weakened the market for wild fish. The number of fishermen who are able to make a living by catching wild salmon has fallen over the years. It will be a matter for regret if the traditional skills of the fishermen and their unique way of life are lost altogether.

impeded at some point during their journey upstream. But most salmon start their journey home well ahead of spawning and most complete by far the greater part of it with weeks or months to spare. Most salmon are therefore in a position to make sound decisions at leisure or to take time to correct false steps made in error. They can do so long before the proximity of spawning itself might intervene to limit their options or to impair their judgement. By the same measure, any straying that takes place amid the final confusions of spawning will again tend to be local rather than extensive. As a general rule, straying will occur more often between adjacent populations than between distant ones.

Various theoretical models have been developed to describe the exchange of strayers and the flow of genetic material among populations for a variety of plausible situations. The basis of these models is complex and need not concern us here. But in their final form they conform to common sense and appear quite straightforward. In a graphic metaphor, the elegant stepping-stone model describes how genes (or straying fish) from one population are more likely to be contributed (or to stray) to an adjacent rather than a distant population.

Intuitively, the stepping-stone metaphor seems likely to describe the relationship between salmon populations separated by discontinuities. For example, from the spawning salmon's point of view, river catchments are isolated from one another by a barren expanse of sea water in which spawning cannot take place. So in this case, the discrete stepping-stones required by the model seem to be in place. For fish that can make even part of their planned journey home successfully, straying is likely to be more common among stepping-stones that lie close together than among those that are greater distances apart. And indeed, genetic studies suggest that this is the case. Along the Scottish coast, for example, river populations in the most distantly spaced catchments are most genetically different; closely spaced catchments are more similar to one another.

To a lesser extent, stepping-stones also seem to be in place within river catchments. The yes-or-no decisions river entrants must make are echoed in the decisions required of fish homing to particular tributaries. We saw in Chapter 5 that many Girnock salmon are capable of homing with this degree of accuracy, and there is no reason to suppose that Girnock fish are at all unusual in this respect. The salmon that home to different tributaries to spawn there are isolated by their diverging paths. So, once again, a stepping-stone array of discontinuities exists.

On the other hand tributaries, unlike rivers, are not separated by clear reaches of barren space. The main river stem that connects tributaries with one another is available for spawning, and it is often used intensively. In river stems and near the junctions of tributaries with rivers, obvious discontinuities and clear stepping-stones do not exist. Even so, fish that can complete most of their journey home would again be expected to stray more often over small distances than over longer ones. Even in the absence of clear discontinuities, distance alone will tend to keep breeding populations of homing fish apart.

In addition to geography and distance, there are two further factors that separate spawning populations. Time plays a role. As we saw previously, peak spawning time

This spawner carries a coded wire microtag. The microtag is located in the nasal cartilage and it cannot be seen. Because of this, the adipose fin (the small rounded fin that is located on the back between the tail and the dorsal fin) is always removed from smolts as microtagging is carried out. The fin does not grow again and its absence indicates that the fish is microtagged. The adipose fin is missing in the fish pictured, although a small remnant can be seen. Netsmen and anglers are asked to report captures of salmon without adipose fins so that the microtag can be removed and decoded to discover where the fish has come from.

differs among river populations. Even within catchments, spawning is often completed in streams distant from the sea before spawners waiting in the lower river are in spawning condition. For fish that may stray between or within catchments, mismatches in sexual development will impede successful spawning. Finally, as we know already, male parr sire a large part of each new generation. These parr spawn without having visited the ocean – indeed, without ever having moved any great distance from the site of their own emergence. The parrs' capacity for straying from their own population to any other is correspondingly reduced. Parr tended to propagate their genes near the places where they acquired them.

As we have seen, nearly all the most useful information on salmon breeding populations has come from the study of genes that code for proteins. This was the only approach possible for many years but it had several important limitations. First, the number of genes that it was possible to study was rather small. Secondly, protein genes represent only one of several types of genetic variation that exist. Both these impasses have been eased to some extent by recent studies that have extended our knowledge of salmon genetics using new DNA technology to probe other types of genetic variation and to provide additional information. These new studies have indicated that the general picture of populations formed on the basis of previous studies of the proteins is accurate. In short, separate breeding populations of salmon exist, although their genetic isolation is not total. Genetic material is exchanged among populations but the extent of exchange is not great enough to make them all the same.

The third problem with the genetic information that is available to us now is so important that it is worth considering in some detail. The types of genetic variation for which we have most information are usually supposed to be without effect on fishes' lives (although, as we have seen, the MEP-2 gene may be a special exception). Some types of genes however, make a great deal of difference to the types of lives that salmon lead. In fact, salmon, like all other creatures, differ from one another in every aspect of their lives – in their appearance, in their development and in their behaviour. As we saw before, there can be only two underlying causes for all this variation. One is the differences in the conditions in which individuals live, and the other part (however large or small it may be) is the differences in the genetic make-up that each individual inherits from its parents. In everyday life, it is this aspect of genetics that most people recognise and respond to – the genes that can be clearly seen to matter.

For example, farmers have altered livestock populations by selective breeding for many thousands of years, working intuitively and with no formal knowledge of science. Farmers have changed breed standards greatly by building on differences in the genetic make-up of individuals originally obtained from wild populations of poultry, cattle or sheep, for example. And as would be expected, selective breeding of fish is also possible. In Asia, for example, selective breeding of ornamental carp has a long history. Genetic improvement of salmon was not attempted until relatively recently, but already specially selected strains of salmon are used exclusively in aquaculture.

In the same way, anglers and fishery managers recognise that wild salmon in their various streams and rivers differ in a number of obvious way. Relying on intuition, rivermen have believed that the differences observed are passed from generation to generation and – therefore, of course, that the differences are genetically determined. In addition, rivermen have believed that the genetic properties involved could be transferred from place to place. Salmon eggs have frequently been transferred from one river to another in attempts to alter existing fisheries permanently in some desired way. For example, the progeny of large fish have been introduced to rivers with a natural run of small adults in attempts to increase the average size of the fish caught. The progeny of spring-running fish have been introduced in attempts to establish spring runs where none existed before.

It has never been proved with scientific rigour whether or not these manipulations have achieved the intended effects. The failures – if they truly were failures – will have resulted from either of two causes. On the one hand, rivermen may have been in error in believing that the differences noted were caused by genes, in which case, the introduced fish will have changed their character to match environmental conditions in their new home, and will have become indistinguishable from the native fish. Alternatively, it may be that special salmon transferred from one location to another are unable to contribute their special genes permanently to their adoptive population. Perhaps by their very nature, unusual genetic lifestyles are not freely transferable among locations; lifestyles that work well in one set of local conditions are inclined to fail elsewhere.

CHAPTER 10

Why Populations Matter

In 1938, W.J.M. Menzies of the Fishery Board for Scotland visited Canada to address an international conference on the conservation of salmon. Following the main meeting, informal discussions took place among some of the principal salmon scientists of the day. A record was kept of these talks and it was included in the official account of the conference[10]. In his opening contribution to the discussions, Menzies showed startling prescience in a passage that reads as follows:

> It is true that even if specific local stocks [of salmon] for individual rivers do exist we cannot expect that the distribution will be absolutely perfect and that a few fish will not occasionally enter, possibly temporarily, a wrong river. But if we can quote as between different rivers and in strictly comparable circumstances differences of weight, condition, distribution of age groups, smolt lengths and ages, and types of parr growth, then I do submit that the only explanation can be the existence of separate biological units in each river which, through the course of time and in response to the local environment, have developed these characteristics. When such features are reinforced by more equivocal circumstances such as the variations in the times of run and in the proportions of different age classes as well as the total number of salmon in each river, any other conclusion seems to be impossible.

Using his imagination to make sense of what he saw around him, Menzies had stepped forward more than 50 years. Indeed, he had anticipated several of the most important messages we have tried to develop so far in this book. Menzies also anticipated one of the messages we will try to develop in this chapter, when he remarked that the local environment might have gradually shaped the variation he observed. His views were not couched in particularly genetic terms, and today he would have phrased things differently. He would have said something like 'natural selection appears to have made populations of salmon genetically adapted to their local environments'. He also pitched his views at the level of the river catchment, whereas today, he might well have gone even further to consider that separate populations of salmon also exist within rivers.

Oddly enough, the opinions that Menzies expressed with such conviction were not found so compelling by others. We know this because his message was widely

10. J.W. Menzies. In 'The Migration and Conservation of Salmon'. Publication of the American Association for the Advancement of Science No. 8 (1939).

ignored in fisheries management for many years. The practice of moving young salmon and their genes in large numbers, over great distances and without regard has continued until this day. Only within the last decade has his view re-emerged, and it is now accepted by many biologists and fishery managers. Why has this change come about? And why, when Menzies was able to form his views so long ago, have his successors laboured so hard to reach the same conclusions?

Menzies' ideas failed to win acceptance because he could not support them with the necessary evidence. Of course, he was not in a position to construct a more convincing case than he did. He had exhausted all the possibilities offered by the biological techniques available at the time. A much stronger case for the importance of populations in the management of salmon fisheries can be presented today, on the basis of recent research. Modern methods have produced much of the missing evidence and, although they have not done so yet, they are capable of producing it all.

We have seen how separate breeding populations of salmon do exist, just as Menzies believed. This is of the greatest importance in itself. You may recall the first lesson of school algebra – that xs and ys are to be considered distinct and that they must be reckoned separately. In the same way, salmon must be categorised and tallied according to their membership of particular populations. Only when this is done is it possible to focus clearly on the numbers. Only then is it possible to discover how salmon fisheries are put together from the separate contributions made by different popultions. In short, the structure of populations and the structure of the fisheries – in the sea, along the coast and in rivers – are closely linked. The fisheries cannot be managed adequately without a thorough understanding of both. What is more, if populations are genetically adapted to their own local environments, as Menzies believed, then populations and population structure are doubly important.

Adaptations develop in many different types of creatures as natural selection acts over the passing generations. In any set of circumstances, individuals perform differently. In some circumstances, individuals of particular genetic types prosper at the expense of others. In the end, the fortunes of individuals determine their ability to produce offspring. Successful fish pass successful genes to their progeny. So, in each new generation, the balance of genes and the balance of genetic types is biased towards those that proved most successful before. In the new generation, the same selective forces may act again, amplifying small changes produced previously. New forces may act to produce genetic changes of other kinds. In isolated populations, small genetic changes will accumulate gradually over successive generations. And small genetic differences among populations will become more pronounced.

Natural selection cannot hone and polish populations of salmon, and make them distinct as well, unless the groups are at least partially genetically isolated from one another. If isolation does not exist, the distinctions that selection chisels out in one generation will become scrambled by interbreeding in the next. We have seen how the isolating framework for selection (the stepping-stones of

Net and coble fishery in the Kyle of Sutherland, the estuary of the Rivers Shin, Carron and Oykel. A sweep-net is run off the coble to enclose salmon passing on the tide. The nearer figure in the distance is leading one end of the sweep-net towards the coble – the line of floats that supports the net can be seen running to the right. The oarsmen have almost completed their circuit and the net is almost closed. A second sweep-net is stowed on the stern of the moored coble ready for use.

Both ends of the net are drawn together and hauled ashore, bringing in the catch.

The net and coble fishery on the River Tweed. The catch has been secured. The fishermen are preparing to shoot the net again. Net and coble fisheries are one of the oldest of the traditional salmon fishing methods.

population structure) is in place, and how genetic isolation is a commonplace.

Natural selection does not actually initiate change. It operates by shaping new forms out of variations that already exist. We know that every salmon differs genetically from every other one – that each one is genetically unique. We also know that populations differ genetically from one another. So the raw material for selection, genetic variation, does exist. Even so, selection cannot operate until it can gain purchase on some distinguishing feature of individuals' lives. Selection exerts its effects by testing individuals over the whole course of their lives and grading them for performance. We have seen how the lives of individual salmon are conducted in any of a wide variety of different ways, and how some salmon populations perform in a characteristic manner that distinguishes them from other populations. So if any part of this variation in performance is genetically determined, selection is well placed to act.

The habits of salmon, like all other animals, must be consistent with the environment in which they live. The range of environments experienced by salmon populations world-wide is very varied. Even within Britain, they range from the warm, stable chalk streams of southern England to the turbulent waters of the Scottish mountains where temperatures vary greatly over the seasons. So is every salmon equally suited to life in any of these places, or are the salmon that live in particular places better suited to live there than anywhere else? Has natural selection honed the genes of local populations to match performance with environmental conditions? Even today, there is little more direct evidence to answer this question than when Menzies pondered the same points.

Juvenile salmon in Rocky Brook and Sabbies River, both tributaries of the Southwest Miramichi in Canada, have different body shapes. Rocky Brook fish are more streamlined and have bigger fins. The environments of the two streams differ markedly: Rocky Brook is faster and rougher than Sabbies River. The differences in body shape might be supposed to result from either of two effects. On the one hand, each Rocky Brook fish might develop its streamlining and grow large fins anew, as a result, for example, of having to take exercise more frequently in faster-flowing water. On the other hand, streamlining might be an adaptation to life in fast water which is built into to the genes of Rocky Brook fish. In fact, the latter explanation was supported when these competing possibilities were tested by experiment.[11] The differences between Rocky Brook and Sabbies River fish were still evident when fish of both groups were reared in a standard hatchery environment.

We know that cold-blooded animals such as fish are especially sensitive to temperature and that temperature is one of the most important components of their environment. So in searching for further evidence of local adaptation, a consideration of temperature and genetics might be a promising place to start. You will recall that in our discussion of the MEP-2 gene in Chapter 8 we saw how temperature appears to dictate the distribution of the alternative forms of the MEP-2 gene among populations across the world. This alone suggests that natural selection might be at work; the different MEP-2 genes may make the salmon that bear them more successful in cooler or warmer streams.

Growth and maturity are aspects of performance that are crucial to each fish's ability to produce offspring. We saw that both these processes differ in some respects among fish carrying the different MEP-2 genes. It may be that natural selection acts against fish carrying one or other of the MEP-2 genes. It may also be that selection favours different genes in cool or warm conditions, because the fish carrying different genes perform differently at particular temperatures. This would result in populations that are better adapted to local environments because of the balance of MEP-2 genes that their members now bear. If this tentative explanation is correct, it links populations and local genetic adaptation with important characteristics like growth and sea age at maturity. Both are important biological qualities, of course, but they are also of obvious interest from a practical, riverman's point of view.

---

11. B.E. Riddell, W.C. Leggett and R.L. Saunders. 'Evidence of adaptive polygenic variation between two populations of Atlantic salmon (*Salmo salar*) native to tributaries of the S.W. Miramichi River, N.B.' *Canadian Journal of Fisheries and Aquatic Sciences* (1981) 38: 321–333.

In this same context, a study carried out in Norway examined differences in the time at which adult salmon return from the ocean. Salmon returning to the Figga and Imsa Rivers appear in the fishery along the Norwegian coast at different times of year: Figga fish in early summer and Imsa fish in late summer and autumn. This difference in timing might come about because Figga and Imsa fish experience different river environments while they are still young; or it might reflect the particular genetic make-ups of Figga and Imsa salmon. In fact, it was shown by experiment that the latter was the correct explanation.[12] The return timing of Figga and Imsa adults was still different after groups of fish from both rivers had been reared together in a hatchery, before being tagged and released as smolts. So perhaps differences in the timing of the adults' return reflect local genetic adaptations.

These few pieces of information are of great interest. Taken together with all the other information on salmon populations, they strengthen the case for believing that local genetic adaptations do exist. The case for local adaptation still cannot be considered proved on the basis of what we know, but a riverman, using good judgement and natural caution, would consider, as Menzies did, that 'any other conclusion seems to be impossible'.

Cause and effect can easily be seen in the Canadian study. Selection pushes fish that are not genetically predisposed to slimness towards failure in fast-flowing streams; the effect of this is a locally adapted population that is genetically predisposed to slimness. On the other hand, it is not so easy to imagine how cause and effect might be linked in the Norwegian study. Perhaps Imsa and Figga smolts leave their rivers at different times. Perhaps Imsa smolts travel further out into the ocean than Figga fish and take correspondingly longer to make their way back. Or perhaps Imsa fish are advantaged by delaying their return to what is a small river without holding pools. But, if this is so, why do Figga fish return earlier? And, pursuing the same question further, why do some salmon populations return to the large spring-fishing rivers as much as a year before they spawn? Why do fish like these take so long to complete the final stage of their journey? Why do they leave the sea when they might remain there, as other types of salmon do? Unfortunately, it is not possible to provide satisfactory answers to any of these seemingly simple questions, for a number of reasons.

To survive until spawning, each salmon (with the exception of male parr) must perform adequately in a sequence of quite distinct environments – streams, rivers, estuaries, coastal seas and the ocean. The qualities of lifestyle that distinguish individual salmon or salmon populations are the final result of long sequences of separate events played out in all these environments. For life to be even a modest success, each fish must perform adequately at every stage of its life. Failure at any stage has the same result. In the final reckoning, a fish that dies the day before spawning is no more successful than one that dies the day after hatch. Among those fish that do pass all the various tests, some will perform better or worse than others, contributing greater or lesser numbers of progeny (and genes) to the next generation.

12. L.P. Hansen and B. Jonsson. 'Evidence of a genetic component in the seasonal return pattern of Atlantic salmon, *Salmo salar* L'. *Journal of Fish Biology* (1991) 38: 251–258.

Trying to make sense of the lifestyles of salmon and trying to compare them poses all the problems faced by a buyer trying to judge the merits of competing audio systems. The most obvious qualities – matt black finish and a graphic equaliser – are not necessarily the most important. The inquisitive buyer might wish to consider how each system is put together. But most of the components are hidden from sight and glimpses of single components tell him little about how they are integrated or how the whole system is designed. In fact, the only practical test of performance is how well the separate units – player, amplifier and speakers – work together to produce their effect.

In salmon, too, the most obvious differences in life-style may not be the most telling. Again, the components and connections of each facet of lifestyle are hidden deep in the physiology or behaviour of individuals. Links between causes that started early in life and effects produced later are obscured by the complexity of the connections between the life-cycle's phases. The significance of effects rooted in causes that happened in previous generations is lost in the intervening layers of time. As a result of all this, we should not expect a few random glimpses of the salmon's biology to fall easily into patterns that make obvious sense. Like audio systems, the fishes' lives can only be judged as a whole.

A salmon carcase damaged by a seal. The fish is a fresh-run female. The eggs in the still undeveloped ovaries have been exposed where the fish's throat has been bitten away. Seals eat a wide variety of marine fish species, including salmon. They eat or damage fish that are already trapped in nets – indeed, they are capable of raiding the innermost compartment of bag- or jumper-nets and escaping unharmed. Seals are also capable of catching free-swimming salmon in the sea or in estuaries and, in some places, they can be observed doing so.

For the scientist, experiments are tools that can be used to obtain glimpses behind the surface. The Canadian and Norwegian studies cited above demonstrate how controlled, standard environments can be used to bring genetic differences between populations into sight. However, performance, in all its various aspects, results from the interplay of the genes that fish contain with the environment in which they live. The environments of hatcheries or aquaria are unnatural and they distort fishes' lives. Local genetic adaptations are expressed appropriately only in the environment in which they have evolved. In the end, therefore, differences in performance can only be judged properly in wild fish living in natural streams and rivers. From a practical point of view, the riverman can draw only tentative conclusions from experiments carried out in tanks.

Recent technical developments have made it possible to get around some of these difficulties. In Chapter 7, we saw how the development of new genetic probes had made it possible to tease apart the biology of spawning salmon. We saw how offspring could be assigned to their parents by using the probes to track the transfer of DNA from one generation to the next. But the power of the probes does not end there; DNA can be tracked over longer periods. In particular, the DNA that each individual contains can be tracked onwards to its offspring as well as backwards to its parents. Using the probes, fish can be studied for the duration of their lives and their genes can be followed for even longer. Wild fish can be studied in their natural environment and their genes can be tracked through the generations. The effectiveness of different lifestyles in passing genes from one generation to the next can be tested in nature. This work is only now beginning but, in time, it will fill some of the many remaining gaps in our knowledge.

It is inconceivable however, that a final, definitive account of the population biology of salmon will ever be possible. It would be a mistake to imagine that population structure, the forces of selection and the nature of local adaptations are fixed – that what exists now is in some near perfect, final form. Instead, what we can see now is only a snapshot, one frame in a continuous sequence of changes. Populations are active, living units that change all the time.

The various lifestyles that lend interest to the fisheries exist now because of their success in the past. The balance of the various styles is a measure of how successful each style has been relative to the others. In general, of course, what has happened in the past is quite a good guide to what might happen in the future. However, the conditions in which salmon lead their lives change continually in small ways and, sometimes, larger changes hold sway. Populations have the capacity to accommodate small or slow changes at least, by changing themselves in appropriate ways. In fact, this is their most interesting and important property. So no aspect of the population biology of salmon should be expected to remain the same in the long run. Populations will come to be regarded as a central concept in fishery management, but they will prove to be a challenging, moving target.

CHAPTER 11

Managing Salmon Populations

The discoveries of the Victorian naturalists opened the way for systematic attempts at fishery improvement more than 100 years ago. In the nineteenth century, the desire to increase salmon fisheries was driven in two ways that are still familiar today. The principal aim was to develop the fisheries as fully as possible for economic benefit. Unfortunately, improvement had often become necessary because fisheries had declined in the face of developments and improvements of other kinds. Urbanisation and early industrial methods were not compatible with the clean water and unobstructed rivers that salmon require for life.

In both Europe and North America, industrial development blighted many once-famous rivers for a century or more. Indeed, some fisheries are still affected. Others have recovered as the legacy of industrial problems has been addressed. Most important of all, pure water from clean rivers is now recognised as a valuable resource in itself. Many of the problems that remain for salmon are local and open to local remedy. But others are more general and some are even international. Through acid emissions, for example, industry exerts environmental effects widely and at a great distance. In rivers that are exposed and susceptible to its effects, acid rain eliminates fish life where it falls. As a result, salmon are completely absent now from rivers in large tracts of southern Norway. These rivers tend naturally to acidity because of the geology of their catchments. But industrial emissions from distant sources in Europe have pushed acidity levels beyond the point at which young salmon can survive.

The fortunes of salmon have been affected by changes of other kinds, too. Within the past 50 years, impoundment projects, land drainage, deep ploughing and industrial forestry have changed many river catchments markedly. Impoundment dams stop or hinder the upstream passage of adults and they drown spawning streams and rearing habitat. Drainage schemes speed the transit of rainfall through river catchments, changing stable streams into 'flashy' ones. The sands and silts liberated by deep ploughing clog spawning gravel and inundate the open-pebbled riffles where young salmon live. Poor forestry practice alters water flow through catchments. Preparatory ploughing speeds water flow in the early years. Later, the developing canopy of leaves traps rainfall and slows and reduces its delivery to streams. Unsympathetic planting schemes degrade habitat by

A victim of pollution. This salmon shows the symptoms of haemolytic jaundice. This syndrome was apparently peculiar to the River Don in Aberdeenshire. The syndrome's occurrence was seasonal and intermittent. After an extended period of difficult detective work its cause was traced to two contaminants reaching the river from different sources. Separately the contaminants were without effect, but together they caused the disease. The problem was rectified by improved treatment of waste water from a factory.

depriving streams of light and by crowding out the herbage on which habitat quality depends.

For more than a century now, the plight of salmon has been a subject of remark. Salmon have faced various problems at different times over the years, but the list of hazards appears to have proliferated as time has passed. Concern has also become more widespread. At first, the most important problems and their causes seemed closely and obviously linked. Now concern has extended to embrace the fisheries of apparently pristine rivers in remote places. In the oceans, the fisheries of west Greenland and the Faroe Islands failed before their recent closure. This failure was not the inevitable consequence of the fisheries' own actions, as might be supposed. Instead, the fish and the fisheries appear to have been overwhelmed by oceanographic changes. Salmon appear to be in special need of support, and following the suspension of the ocean fisheries, it is in rivers where the most telling support can now be offered.

All salmon fisheries can be increased by one means or another. Irrespective of other interests, the foremost aim must be to optimise the numbers of spawning fish, such that each new generation is founded at its full strength. Many different approaches to this are possible, but they all fall into one of only two broad categories. In the first, measures are taken to regulate the numbers or type of adult fish killed, with the aim of conserving potential spawners and their progeny to the

Part of the channel of the River Garry dries out from time to time below an impoundment dam for power generation. Salmon cannot live in conditions like these, not even temporarily.

benefit of the fishery in future years. Much of the informal etiquette that anglers have developed is directed to this end, and most of the fisheries regulations are directed in the same way. Regulation has reached its most sophisticated form in the North American rivers. Here, fishing methods and the number and size of the salmon that may be retained by anglers are closely prescribed and set in accordance with the state of particular fisheries. Measures like these are a valuable management tool, and restrictions on current fisheries undoubtedly affect future ones in a positive way. In general, measures to regulate rod fishing have not been used as a matter of routine in Europe, but in future, restraints will inevitably become necessary as angling effort increases and the catch begins to exceed the ability of salmon populations to produce excess fish. We will return to this subject in the next chapter.

The second category of approaches to fishery management involves positive measures to improve fisheries directly by increasing the numbers of fish entering them. The most extreme version of this approach is salmon ranching, as practised in Baltic Sweden. The progeny of brood-stock caught up in rivers are raised in captivity until they become smolts and then released in large numbers into rivers that have been targeted for enhancement. Some of the fish are caught in the fisheries of the Baltic Sea. Later, ranched fish return to the river where they were released and contribute to the rod fishery there. It is not regarded as particularly important that ranched salmon should go on to contribute to the establishment of the next generation of wild juveniles in rivers – indeed, if all the ranched fish should be caught at sea or by the rods, the ranching exercise would be judged a special success.

Salmon ranching is a modern embellishment of traditional hatchery practice. Hatcheries are a tangible and satisfying way of managing salmon rivers and they are used almost everywhere. The case for hatcheries was first espoused by Frank Buckland, the Victorian eccentric, who numbered salmon and salmon fisheries among his many diverse interests. Buckland was an enthusiastic proponent of the new techniques of fish culture being developed in his day as a means of enhancing salmon production in rivers. His attitude to salmon was very down-to-earth. He viewed them principally as a source of wholesome food and, as Inspector of Salmon Fisheries, his efforts were focused on increasing the productivity of English rivers. In essence, his approach was to remove the barriers to upstream movement posed by the weirs and dams that had proliferated on England's rivers and to use fish-culture methods to hasten the re-establishment of juvenile salmon in water opened up again to adults.

Buckland used hatcheries to compensate for the effects of past problems. Crucially, he was careful to ensure that the original causes of the problems had been removed or lessened before hatchery work began. The hatchery techniques that he used to restore fisheries were exactly the same as those that are used so widely today. All hatchery work follows the same simple pattern. Adults are caught up and stripped and the fertilised eggs are incubated in hatchery trays over the winter months. In spring, the fry are planted out just before they commence feeding, often but not always into the same catchment from which their parents were taken. At this point, the fry are abandoned to make their own way in life.

All streams gather sediment from their banks and transport it seawards over long periods of time. In this photograph a recent meander has cut at the base of a moraine of fine sands and gravel deposited by a glacier during the last ice age. Several hundred tonnes of material has been washed into the stream over a short period of time. The face of the moraine is not sufficiently stable to support vegetation and erosion continues. Because the stream's gradient is relatively steep the material has been dispersed quickly rather than accumulating locally on the stream bed. Electrofishing has shown that substantial numbers of salmon and trout still inhabit the stream section pictured in the foreground.

A conifer plantation that had overgrown this stream has been cut back as a fisheries management measure. Vegetation is absent or sparse on the bank-side where light has been excluded until recently by the canopy of trees. The stream has been widened and the banks have been destabilised where lack of light has killed the herbage. Prior to clearance the stream contained few fish. Now a programme of stocking with salmon fry has begun.

The Veazie Dam on the Penobscot River in Maine during the spring run-off in April. Towards the turn of the century the commercial catch of salmon on the Penobscot was almost 20,000 fish each year. By 1948 the catch had declined to 40 as a result of the obstruction of passage to the spawning areas and water pollution. Salmon were never completely lost to the river. Since 1948 a series of measures have been taken to restore the river and to reinstate a worthwhile salmon fishery. Today, several thousand salmon return to the Penobscot annually as a result of hatchery-based programmes. These programmes continue, with the ultimate aim of establishing vigorous self-sustaining runs of wild salmon.

Trays of alevins in a hatchery. The alevins have crowded to the edges and corners of the trays because of their aversion to light. When the fish are not being tended, the covers that can be seen on the left are used to exclude light from the trays. In darkness (which mimics the natural conditions within the redd), the alevins remain quiescent and spread themselves evenly over the surface of the tray.

Most hatcheries stock extra fry into rivers and streams that already contain the progeny of natural spawning. There is usually no means of distinguishing the hatchery fry from the wild ones and, in most circumstances, it is not possible to find out just how effective hatcheries are. In special situations, however, hatchery fry can be shown to survive and hatchery techniques can be shown to be inherently sound – indeed, this would be expected given their simplicity. However, attempting to make a substantial (or even an appreciable) difference to salmon production in the open reaches of a large river (or even a small one) is a daunting task. The principles behind hatchery work must be considered fully to ensure that it is carried out to very best effect.

As we have seen, fry die in countless numbers after they emerge onto the stream bed, as a result of their failure in the competition for living space. The greater the number of hatching fry, the greater the proportion that die. The requirements of hatchery fry are the same as those of their wild counterparts; so in locations that are already adequately stocked by natural spawning, planting hatchery fry will not produce an increase in the number of fish surviving to become parr. To be given any chance of achieving its intended effect, a hatchery must be used strategically – like a rapier rather than a bludgeon. Attention must focus on those places where the number of naturally spawned fry is lowest – but only when the number of fry is too low to ensure that all the stream habitat that is available is actually used.

Even when these conditions are met, the results of stocking may not fulfil the expectations of the impatient or the over-ambitious. Calderwood pointed out many years ago[13] that catching up adult brood-stock for the hatchery deprives the same fish of the chance to contribute to natural spawning. So if hatchery fry are turned back into the places from which their parents were procured, the expected gain is equivalent to the difference between egg mortality in streams and hatcheries. Eggs in streams are exposed to the full rigours of nature while those in hatcheries are protected and, as a rule, the survival of hatchery eggs is the greater. However, Calderwood also pointed out that, even in a small, modestly productive river, the number of females that a hatchery might accommodate is only a small proportion of all the females in the river. So, after planting out the fry, the effect that the improved survival of the hatchery eggs has on the river's stock of juveniles will be determined by what small portion of all the spawning stock was caught up for stripping. In uniformly well-stocked streams, hatchery work cannot be expected to improve appreciably on nature. Hatcheries have a worthwhile role to play but only where gaps exist in the natural distribution of salmon fry.

Good hatcheries are therefore used strategically. In some cases, strategy is meticulously devised and planned. In others, an intuitive strategy develops, based on long experience. But by whatever means they come about, the best strategies have two common aims. First the causes of the problems that require attention are identified and, if possible, rectified. Then the progeny of adults procured in places where they are numerous are used to fill gaps in the natural distribution of fry. However, even this simple approach is fraught with difficulties for those concerned to get the best results from their efforts – or, at least, to avoid doing harm.

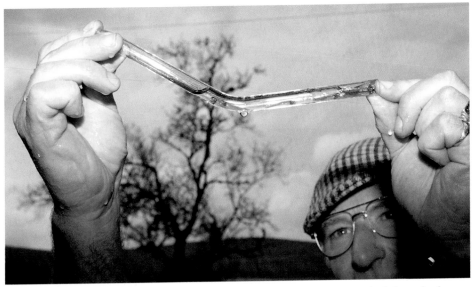

Checking the condition of alevins. A sample of young fish is drawn into a crooked glass tube for ease of viewing. These alevins have absorbed most of their yolk-sac and they will be ready for planting out soon.

This fry has almost absorbed its yolk-sac. At this stage, alevins move actively away from light. Usually, fish like these would still be buried deep within the gravel of the redd.

A hatchery unit of several thousand fry ready for stocking out. The fish are active and free-swimming and capable of fending for themselves now.

Planting out salmon fry at the end of May. These young fish are from eggs stripped in November and incubated in hatchery trays over the winter months. The eggs hatched in April but the alevins were retained until the yolk-sac had been fully absorbed. Research has shown that, with careful stocking, 50 per cent of fry can survive the initial hazards of stream life.

Thus, the incautious may view the distribution of young salmon in catchments, and the gaps in their distribution, in terms of geography alone. But the biology of the fish in question is of equal concern. Thus salmon populations are also organised by geography. It follows, therefore, that gaps in the distribution of salmon can be viewed equally as weaknesses in local populations. Looking at matters in this way emphasises an important point. All the information and the arguments presented in previous chapters have led us to the view that salmon populations differ from one another in important respects that determine the style of life that their members lead, and ultimately, the extent of their members' success. Hatchery work must therefore be more than an exercise in numbers. Hatcheries should aim to support fisheries in the long term, by establishing or supporting self-sustaining natural populations of salmon. Good hatchery work supports population structure by delivering fry of the appropriate type to particular places.

As we saw in Chapter 8, the diversity that exists between and within the fisheries of different rivers appears to reflect the fact that particular genetic types of salmon are more successful in some places than they are in others. In other words, the populations that salmon comprise appear to differ from one another in the sorts of genetic adaptations they contain. In general, special adaptations will be of advantage in particular environments where fish that bear them will be favoured over those that do not. Special adaptations that favour life in one environment will not be preferred in another. As a result, hatchery-reared progeny moved from one place to another may well fail to take in their new location.

Unfortunately, the size of local populations and the boundaries between them cannot be described precisely. But it is known that adjacent populations are more similar genetically than those that are greater distances apart. Hatchery work should aim to strengthen local populations without eroding differences among them. So good practice requires that movements of fry are made over the smallest distances that are consistent with the task in hand. In practical terms, working like this – with the natural grain – is likely to prove more effective than any other approach. Moving fry that are genetically adapted to a special environment to a new location may not meet with permanent success.

However, hatchery work has to address a range of problems, and each problem invites a different solution. For example, the extinction of salmon populations may affect whole catchments or even groups of catchments. In these circumstances, restoration demands that fry be moved in from distant populations. In the absence of better-adapted native competitors, fish from any donor population may be able to establish a new fishery or to restore a traditional one. On the other hand, a well-chosen source of fry that attempts to match the donor population to its new environment will hasten the point at which the new population becomes self-sustaining.

The New England salmon fisheries were decimated or eradicated long ago as a result of industrial development along the rivers. The Connecticut River, for example, runs for 650km south through New England to reach the sea in Long Island Sound. It is the southernmost refuge of Atlantic salmon in North America. The river is reputed to have supported extremely prolific runs of salmon before the construction of dams was started to provide water power for industry. About 1800, a major construction project of this type excluded returning adult salmon from all their spawning streams in Vermont and New Hampshire. Predictably, the Connecticut River's runs of salmon had almost ceased within four years and salmon were absent within a decade or so. In fact, all the New England rivers suffered in a similar way at about the same time, although salmon were never completely lost in some.

A series of projects designed to restore salmon to the New England rivers was started in the late 1960s and the programme continues to this day. It was always going to be a challenge because the rivers are at or near to the natural southern limit of the salmon's range. Low latitudes coupled with a continental climate result in summer water temperatures that approach or, in places, exceed the lethal limit for salmon. It is quite likely, therefore, that New England's original salmon were special in being able to exploit such a marginal environment. However, these types of fish had been reduced everywhere and made extinct in most of the rivers. It was necessary therefore to base restoration on fish brought in from a variety of rivers further north. These salmon have gained a foothold in their new environment, although it has required an immense effort to achieve this, using hatchery work in all its forms. Even now, continued hatchery support will be essential if New England's new salmon populations are to be made secure.

Most hatcheries operate on a lesser scale, enhancing populations in catchments that support good or moderate fisheries. No catchments are fully populated by fry and even the best fisheries can be improved by hatchery work. Each year, for example, reaches of stream around the very periphery of catchments, beyond the range of the most travelled spawners, go unfilled by fry. Gaps in the uptake of habitat result when spawning populations suffer a temporary weakness. In spawning seasons that are unusually dry, for example, spawners may fail to penetrate streams in adequate numbers to replenish them fully. Even where they are numerous, they require spawning gravel to construct their redds. This is distributed unevenly along streams and rivers and, as a result, the distribution of redds and later of fry is also uneven.

Fry disperse away from the redds after emergence. But this dispersal is not extensive or rapid and gaps in the distribution of fry are filled out only slowly. Density-dependent mortality is highest soon after emergence. As each new year-class diminishes in number, it loses the capacity to continue filling voids. In all streams, therefore, some part of all the habitat is never fully and continuously used by parr and, later on, all streams produce fewer smolts than they might. Hatchery work can fill these gaps. In its most elegant refinement, hatchery work maximises smolt production by smoothing the distribution of each new year-class through all the available habitat and at the earliest stage of life. In many situations, no great increase in the adult catch may result from planting fry in this way, for the reasons that Calderwood identified. But later, returning hatchery fish become capable of replacing themselves many times over. As adults, they will home to the locations where they were released. And as spawners, they will make good the gaps in the distribution of fry identified a generation before.

Of course, the most sophisticated approach is unrealistically demanding when applied year after year to large river catchments. But two things can ease the burden of the task considerably where time and labour are scarce. First, rather than expending inadequate resources evenly over entire catchments, priorities can be set. Particular components of the fishery can be targeted for improvement by concentrating hatchery support on specific populations. Secondly, a rolling programme of support will be effective. In most streams, smolts leave fresh water in two or more groups, spread over the same number of years. The effects of hatchery work carried out in a single year will be spread in the same way. In addition, adults return to most streams after a variable number of years at sea. So the benefits of a single year's hatchery work will be spread over an even greater number of spawning years. Considered narrowly – in terms of the fishery alone – it might be considered disappointing that the benefits of a year's work should be dissipated in this way. But in terms of supporting populations rather than attempting to improve fisheries directly, the operation will be judged successful.

In 1993, world-wide production of farmed salmon was 270,000 tonnes with a first sale value of about $1,000,000,000.

CHAPTER 12

Farmed Salmon

It is only 25 years since the salmon-farming industry began, as a result of pioneering development work carried out in Norway. From small beginnings, the industry has spread to other countries and increased vastly in size. It now produces more than 200,000 tonnes of salmon annually. Salmon has become a world commodity and farming is a major international industry. Arguably, however, the industry's most telling impact has been on a more local scale. Salmon farming underpins the economies of many fragile communities scattered around the North Atlantic seaboard.

The advent of salmon farming has had profound effects on the fortunes of wild fish. The most obvious of these have been beneficial. The continuous supply of salmon to the world market in large quantities has eroded the premium prices paid for wild salmon in former years. As a result, many previously marginal fisheries have been made unprofitable. Pressure on wild salmon from commercial fishing has diminished in estuaries and on the coasts and, although drift-net fisheries still exist in Irish and English waters, most legal fishing has now ceased (at least temporarily) on the ocean feeding grounds. These changes have ensured that more salmon have run rivers in recent years than would otherwise have been the case. Reduced commercial catches should have meant more fish to the rods and later, more fish on the spawning fords. Unfortunately, this has not always proved to be the case; sometimes the expected improvements have been offset by contrary changes of other kinds.

The principles of commercial salmon farming are straightforward. The fish are grown to convert food that can be obtained at relatively low cost into salmon flesh of greater value. To do this, salmon eggs are hatched and the resulting fish are held in culture for the whole of their lives. Some are held until they become sexually mature and their progeny are used to restart the farming cycle. Salmon farming comprises two subsidiary industries, each of which is based on one of the two main phases of the life cycle: the period of juvenile growth in fresh water and the period of adult marine growth.

The rearing of juvenile salmon is carried out in tank-farms fed by fresh water drawn from wells, streams or rivers or in net-pens moored in lakes. Fish are grown in fresh water for as brief a time as possible – usually a single year – until, as smolts, they are able to survive in sea water. These smolts are transported from fresh-water

Starting the day's work on a salmon farm. Floating net-pens vary in size and design but the one pictured here will be about 4m deep and capable of accommodating several thousand growing salmon. In 1993, almost 50,000 tonnes of salmon were harvested in Scotland – an increase of about 30 per cent over 1992 – and 20 million smolts were transferred to sea water for growing on for future harvests. Salmon farming provides employment for more than 1000 people in Scotland, usually in regions where alternative employment is scarce.

rearing units to the sea, sometimes over large distances, using road-tankers, helicopters or well-boats. After transfer, they are reared in net-pens moored in the sea, as so-called growers. Typically, net-pens are grouped in rafts moored to the sea bed in sheltered places only a short distance from shore.

In the eastern North Atlantic, salmon are farmed in Norway, Scotland, the Faroe Islands and Ireland. In the western Atlantic, they are farmed in Maine in the United States and in the Bay of Fundy and Newfoundland in Canada. Atlantic salmon are also reared in British Columbia and in Chile. Of course, Atlantic salmon are not native to the Pacific Ocean and the eastern Pacific supports several salmon species of its own, but the Atlantic salmon is considered a superior species for farming.

In most cases, farming is carried out in areas that are frequented by wild Atlantic salmon. Indeed, most of the salmon rivers of southern and western Norway, western and northern Scotland and western Ireland, and those of the Bay of Fundy and the Gulf of Maine in North America, support smolt-rearing units or are only a short swimming distance from marine cage-rearing sites. Salmon escape from farms at every stage in their development, and this has had direct effects on the numbers of salmon in the sea and in rivers. In many places, natural runs of wild fish are augmented by escaped fish. It might be thought that the presence of these extra salmon would be welcomed by fishermen accustomed or inured to the concept of the put-and-take fishery. In general, however, the aesthetics of salmon fishing have not evolved to accommodate recent developments and escaped salmon are not always welcomed. Indeed, many scientists and fishery managers have expressed concern that, in the long run, the presence of escaped farmed salmon in rivers will prove harmful to wild populations and detrimental to the fisheries they support.

The trained eye can often identify escaped fish instantly without close inspection, but for the average angler who may see only a few fish each year, the lack of practised comparison makes matters more difficult. Even so, many of the signs are fairly clear, and close inspection of the most obvious features will enable the inexperienced angler to identify escaped growers with near certainty. Identifying fish that have escaped from smolt-rearing units is more difficult and it is impossible to identify fish that have escaped in the very early stages of fresh-water life.

Growers usually have a more spotty appearance than wild fish and, often, a corpulent frame. Many recently escaped growers can be recognised on this basis alone. After longer periods at liberty, the same features cease to be so useful. Escaped fish change their form and eventually come to resemble wild fish quite closely. At this stage, the signs that are most helpful in identifying escaped fish result from the imperfect healing of minor wounds and abrasions. Farmed salmon live their lives, both in fresh water and in the sea, under crowded conditions and within the confines of tanks or netting cages. Superficial abrasions of the extremities are common. Damage like this is usually followed by minor infections and this, in turn, leads to scarring. Although the lesions heal and repair with time, recovery is always incomplete and the resulting disfigurement is permanent.

Net-pens in a western Scottish sea loch. Because of their requirement for clean, sheltered sea water, salmon farms are often located in remote, scenic areas. Modern cage designs are not especially obtrusive and well-managed farms do little to detract from the view.

Fallowed net-pens on a fresh-water loch. The smolts that the pens contained until recently have been transferred to the sea. The cages will shortly be recharged with young fish.

As a group, escaped salmon show characteristic deformities in the paired pectoral and pelvic fins, the dorsal fin, the tail, the gill covers and the snout. In most individuals, some or all of these features are reduced or distorted in some way. Erosion of the dorsal fin is a particularly useful feature in identifying escaped fish, since scarring begins early on in life and the results are fairly obvious. The dorsal fin of most escaped fish is reduced and thickened on its leading edge. Wild fish rarely show evidence of similar injury and any fin damage is never so extensive or, in the case of the paired fins, symmetrical.

Of course, these generalisations can only be made by comparing escaped fish with wild ones when they have been classified by some other means. This can be done by examining the growth patterns shown on scales. As we saw in Chapter 3 scales contain a permanent record of each fish's life in a series of growth rings laid down at wide spacing during periods of fast growth and at closer spacing when growth is slow. The scale rings in wild salmon are laid down in characteristic patterns of alternate winter and summer bands. Farmed fish lay down poorly differentiated patterns at wide spacings because they grow unusually uniformly and quickly. In escaped farmed fish these patterns remain recorded in the inner part of the scales. After escape, scale growth patterns change to the form that is typical of wild fish. This part of their lives is recorded on the outer margins of the scale. With the exception of fish that have escaped at a very early stage of life, therefore, escaped farmed fish can be identified from their atypical scale patterns.

Prime wild salmon taken from the sea. An escaped farmed salmon taken from the same catch lies in their midst. The appearance of escaped fish varies. Some will have escaped recently and may even contain the remains of their last meal of pelleted feed. Others will have been at liberty for a year or more. The fish pictured here shows characteristic deformities of the paired fins, the dorsal fin and the tail. These deformities persist after escape and are the result of chronic minor infections in the crowded conditions of tanks or net-pens.

Sampling young fish. Small fish are disabled in an electric field and can be captured with ease. The scientist on the left is operating a portable electric fishing apparatus powered by batteries. Fish swim involuntarily towards the electrode that the operator is holding, over a range of 0.5m or so. When they have been drawn from their hiding places in the stream bed, fish are captured by net. The effects of electric fishing are temporary. Fish recover immediately when they are removed from the electric field, and they can be returned to the stream without harm.

Escaped salmon and wild fish often differ in another important respect. The synthetic pigments added to salmon feed to impart colour to the flesh of farmed fish differ from the red pigments that wild fish accumulate naturally. Although the two types are quite similar, they can be distinguished in the laboratory. Synthetic colourants are expensive and they are not usually given to farmed fish until some time after their transfer to sea water. So the absence of synthetic colourant in the flesh of a salmon caught at liberty does not prove that it is a wild fish. On the other hand, the presence of colourant leaves no room for doubt that the fish is an escaped one.

The pigments a fish contains, its appearance and scale-reading comprise a battery of complementary tests. Together they have revealed most of what is known about the numbers of escaped farmed fish and their distribution at sea and in rivers. In addition, female salmon pass their own pigments to their eggs and, even after emergence from the gravel, young fish contain their mother's pigment for a brief time. When escaped females contain synthetic colourant, their eggs and their alevins also contain it. This has made it possible to track the spawning of escaped females in streams and rivers with some precision.

In Scotland, salmon farming is concentrated on the west coast, in the Hebrides and in the Orkney and Shetland Islands. This is because the indented coastlines of these areas offer a measure of natural protection for marine cage sites. As a matter of convenience, the distribution of the tank-farms and cages used to rear smolts has tended to follow the distribution of marine farming. The eastern coastline of Scotland differs from the west in being open and very exposed to storms. And as a consequence, the east coast has been almost free of sea-cages and few of the eastern rivers have been used to rear smolts.

In recent years, escaped farmed salmon have been widespread – and sometimes common – in the sea, on the coasts and in rivers throughout the north-eastern Atlantic area. Judging by the patterns of growth shown on their scales, many escaped salmon resume their natural life cycle to travel to quite distant parts of the ocean. Indeed, between 20 and 30 per cent of the fish sampled on the ocean feeding grounds north of the Faroe Islands during the winter of 1992–3 had started their lives in farms. Later in their lives, as sexual maturity approaches, escaped salmon show some measure of fidelity to the places from which they escaped – in much the same way as wild salmon form attachments to the places they leave as smolts. In other words, escaped fish home as wild fish do, but towards the site of their loss rather than their point of departure as smolts.

As a result of their homing, escaped salmon are caught more frequently on the coasts and in rivers near areas in which farming is carried out. In 1993 almost half the fish caught in the Norwegian coastal fisheries were of farmed origin. In Scotland, escaped fish are frequently found in the catches of commercial netting stations on the west and north coasts. Their numbers vary from station to station and throughout the season, but in recent years about 20 per cent of the catch in the north and west has been of salmon that have escaped at some stage in their lives. Some have escaped so recently that they still contain the remains of their last fish-farm meal. Many, however, appear to have been a liberty for several

Electric fishing for adult salmon near spawning time on the River Polla in northern Scotland.

months and some for a year or more.

Understandably, many escaped salmon – and especially those that have escaped from sea-cages – are unable to retrace their steps to their freshwater 'homes' on their return from the ocean. So, when increasing sexual development compels them to seek fresh water, fish like these stray into rivers and streams wherever they find themselves. On the other hand, fish that have escaped from fresh-water rearing units do have a general fresh-water target and many may return to the river in which they were once raised.

As would be expected, most escaped farmed fish in Scotland enter the rivers of the west and north to spawn. In 1991, 16 rivers between the Cree in south-west Scotland and the Carron in the north-east were surveyed for salmon fry that contained synthetic colourant. Fry like these (the progeny of female growers) were found in all the rivers examined, with the exception of the Cree itself and the Inver, in Wester Ross. The rivers examined were chosen because they did not support smolt-production farms. So none of the escaped growers had spawned in the rivers because they believed them to be their original 'homes'. As expected, the progeny of escaped growers were most frequent in samples taken from rivers in the heart of fish-farming country. On the other hand, they were also present in the Helmsdale and Carron on the east coast, far from any source of escaped growers.

Overall, 5 per cent of the young salmon in the 16 rivers examined were shown to have been spawned by female growers. This figure was certainly an underestimate because, for one reason or another, about one third of escaped growers did not contain synthetic colourant when the study was carried out. In addition, the figure underestimates the contribution made to spawning by escaped fish other than growers and by male fish. None of the fish that had escaped from smolt-rearing units, for example, was expected to contain colourant and male fish make no contribution to the pigments of their progeny. It seems, therefore, that, in some places, escaped farmed salmon spawn in substantial numbers. While their spawning is centred on the areas in which farming is carried out, it also extends considerably beyond them.

As we have already seen, wild salmon belong to local populations that differ from one another genetically and in the types of lives that their members lead. Genetic differences between populations are reinforced by homing and eroded by the straying of spawners. Many fish do home, as we have seen, but some straying also occurs. Indeed, strayers are probably important in spreading favourable versions of genes from one population to another. On balance, however, the extent of straying has not been great enough in the past to render all salmon populations the same. The natural balance between homing and straying fosters the separate development of local populations, while tempering the effects of isolation with a measure of genetic exchange.

Very few farmed salmon have been bred from original stock procured from local rivers. Indeed, farmers have gone to considerable lengths to found commercial strains of salmon on stock obtained from rivers that contain fish of particular, desired types. In Scotland, for example, many farmed fish have been bred from stock procured originally in Norway. Many more have been derived from stock obtained in the major east coast rivers. In both cases, these choices have been driven by the desire to develop strains of salmon that show good growth coupled with a tendency not to become mature at any early age. The choice of special rivers has been based only on intuition. But by making their choices, salmon farmers have shown that they too believe that salmon populations differ genetically in demonstrably important ways.

We have seen how escaped fish tend to spawn near the places where they escape and that their real genetic origins are distant from these places. The genetic effect of escaped fish on wild populations will therefore be roughly the same as the effect of wild strayers. However, in populations where these escapees occur, the total number of strayers will be pushed beyond natural levels. The effect that the extra strayers have will be determined by their numbers and by the extent to which they differ genetically from the recipient population. The permanence of their effect will be determined by the survival of their progeny.

Favourable genetic material donated by strayers will be assimilated by the recipient population and even propagated in later generations. More often, however, the donated material will prove less appropriate than the material that has been tried and tested there by past generations of wild fish. In these circumstances, the progeny of strayers will be less likely to survive to spawning than the progeny of native fish and the strayers' genetic imput will tend to be eliminated from the population. The most inappropriate material will be eliminated quickly – perhaps even within a generation or two – but less harmful material will persist for much longer.

Crucially, for wild populations of salmon to remain vigorous the rate at which inappropriate genetic material is expelled must exceed the rate at which it accumulates. The rules that govern these processes are complex and unexplored, and it remains to be seen whether natural populations in the streams and rivers that now receive escaped fish regularly are sufficiently robust to absorb these new genetic impacts.

A wild female kelt captured from the River Polla and an escaped farmed fish in similar condition, captured at the same time. The escaped fish shows the fin deformities characteristic of farmed fish. The fish pictured was one of 180,000 growers that had escaped eight months before from a sea-cage site near the river's mouth. The site was destroyed in the course of a storm. It appears that many of the fish that escaped did not survive long enough to spawn. In total, less than 500 of the escaped fish could be accounted for in later years in rivers near to the site of the accident.

Fly fishing on the River Don. A multiplicity of baits and lures are employed to catch salmon. All lures bear an unmistakable resemblance to one or other of the diverse species that salmon prey on at sea. Many theories have been expounded to explain why salmon that do not feed in rivers should take lures at all. There need be no mystery in this matter. Although large salmon may not support themselves on the meagre food resources available in rivers, it is very unlikely that they abandon their former habits completely. Strong feeding responses acquired in the sea are expressed weakly later on, even by fish that are no longer preoccupied with the necessity to feed and grow. The more interesting question is why salmon express their residual feeding responses in patterns that appear so whimsical.

CHAPTER 13

What Now?

In the preceding chapters, we have tried to show how the form that an individual salmon's life takes is determined by its membership of a particular population, and how population structure determines the character of salmon fisheries. We have suggested that an understanding of population structure is essential for good management. For the angler, too, it ought to be evident now that salmon in different rivers, or fish passing through any beat in the course of a season, are not all the same. Salmon taken by anglers from one river, or from one part of a river's stock, cannot be replaced later by others spared from different populations. Furthermore, each fish removed from the river is removed also from its intended place on the redds, its progeny are removed from future fisheries and its genes are withdrawn from the future development of the population to which it belonged.

Anglers are always vociferous in advocating restraint for other salmon-catchers in the interests of conversation. The so-called mixed-stock fisheries on the coasts and at sea are particularly reviled because they bear indiscriminately on salmon whose intended destination is not known. However, it will have become obvious by now that the mixed-stock concept extends to rivers too, since separate populations of salmon exist within single catchments. The dangers inherent in a mixed-stock rod fishery can be tempered if the concepts of population structure are understood and its strictures observed.

Thus, the spring-running component of the stock in Europe's rivers has declined markedly and catches have fallen precipitously in recent years. This is well known and a matter of wide concern. The underlying causes are not fully understood but as we have seen, they appear to relate to natural changes in the distant northern oceans. These changes have affected spring salmon particularly severely.

Of course, some spring salmon are still being caught. Indeed, rather more are being caught than might be expected. When fish are few in number, anglers are able to catch a greater proportion of those that are present. Inadvertently, and unaware of the consequences, anglers appear to act perversely by increasing their efforts to deplete already weakened runs. As a result, on some rivers where the numbers of spring fish have declined most of all, rather more spring salmon are being caught now and retained than is consistent with the long-term interest of the fisheries concerned.

It is easy to understand how anglers fall corporately into this situation without being at all guilty of malice. Most anglers do not catch many fish in a season and believe, correctly, that their own individual efforts are without much effect overall. But individual angling catches mount up. In some circumstances, anglers have jointly proved themselves to be spectacularly successful predators. In recent years, exploitation by the rods on the already weakened spring runs of some southern British fisheries is estimated to have been greater than 50 per cent – and in some cases, much greater.

Effects like these often go unnoticed because most anglers have a restricted view of the whole scene. In general, awareness does not extend beyond the years of personal experience and, in any case, time distorts everyone's recollections. Few anglers have a picture that extends beyond their own preferred rivers, and many are aware only of their own local beats. Moreover, as is well known, rivermen have a well-developed capacity for self-deception. And it is quite simple to rationalise what may be major effects as small, local difficulties that Nature will resolve in due course.

However, a general view that extends to include a broad history of the fisheries is a more telling yardstick. The catch records for some fisheries are contained in private notebooks or ledgers that reach back to the last century. More recently, official figures have been compiled nationally on the basis of catch returns recorded by anglers and submitted at the season's end. In Scotland, catch records have been compiled formally since 1952. The rod-catch figures are collated separately from the net catches and they are summarised by river and by month. A glance at the figures suggests that the seasonal characteristics of the rod fisheries have changed markedly since records were first kept.

These records are a matter of great interest for anglers because they are a factual account of catches. They are also of great interest to fisheries managers because they can be used to speculate about how stock levels have varied over the years. However, caution must be exercised in using them in this way – catches should not be expected to be exactly proportional to stock levels. For example, we have seen already that exploitation rates change as stock levels vary. In addition, angling pressure has increased steadily over the years. Improved transport has put formerly remote fisheries within striking distance of many more anglers. Increased leisure time has made it possible to travel. And increased incomes have made it possible to pay for all the pleasures involved. As a result of these changes, beats that were fished sporadically in the past are now let for the whole season and fished continually. Most important of all, netting effort everywhere has diminished steadily over the years. Until the 1960s, full crews of netsmen worked full fleets of nets for the whole season along the whole of the Scottish coast. Now many stations are not worked at all and many others are worked only over the summer months. And fewer fish to the nets should mean more fish in the rivers.

All these factors would be expected to result in greater catches for the rods, and indeed, rod catches in Scotland's rivers have increased steadily since the beginning of the official record. In fact, catches in recent years have been approximately double those of the early 1950s. This increase might be linked to any of the factors listed above and to others such as improved equipment and better angling technique. The picture looks rosy for anglers – catches are increasing and even now they show no signs of levelling off. At first sight, then, the future looks assured.

Yet, as we know, this general picture obscures two separate sets of figures that bring completely different messages. When catches are considered for each month of the season, it is clear that all the improvement noted in the annual rod catch is due to increases in catches of grilse and summer salmon. Catches of spring fish have declined everywhere, although they too might have been expected to increase, for all the reasons cited above.

February is the first month of the season for many Scottish rivers; in recent years, the February catch has been about 25 per cent of the 1950s average. March, April and May are the prime spring fishing months, catches in these months are now running at between 35 and 40 per cent of the 1950s average. All these declines have occurred quite gradually, although they were exacerbated by stepwise decreases in the late 1960s and again in the early 1990s. The pattern of decline shows no signs of levelling off and nothing suggests that catches of spring fish can be expected to improve spontaneously in the near future.

Of course, it is possible that the declining catch of spring salmon is linked in some way to the increases in the catch of grilse and summer fish. Perhaps potential spring fish have altered their habits for some reason, to run a month or two later, as summer salmon, or six months or so earlier, as grilse. Certainly, this idea is attractive in its simplicity. If this kind of reciprocation does occur, then those rivers that had formerly supported the purest spring fisheries would be expected to show the greatest compensatory increases in the summer catch.

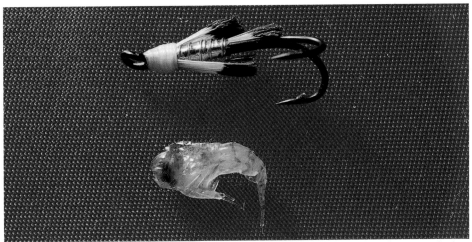

A shrimp-like crustacean obtained from the stomach of a salmon captured in the ocean feeding grounds and a salmon fly. The fly was tied by Rick Connolly of Fochabers as an imitation. The fly has been given the name 'Trigger', in the expectation that it will stimulate half-remembered feeding responses from salmon lying in rivers. The fly is tied on a size 12 double, and it is still unproven!

A nineteenth-century dam constructed to provide water power for a factory nearby. The dam obstructs the passage of migratory fish totally. Even if fish were capable of attempting the face of the dam, the vertical rampart at its summit cannot be surmounted. Unfortunately, the construction of dams like these was widespread in the past, when the requirements of migratory fish were not understood or considered unimportant. The factory powered by this dam was closed some years ago and demolished later. No trace of it exists, but the dam remains.

The catch records show the Dee to have been the premier spring fishery among all the Scottish rivers and probably the best in the world. Indeed, the Dee still holds this position, although spring catches have declined there as they have elsewhere. But an examination of the Dee catch records shows that the missing spring fish have not materialised as catches of summer salmon or grilse. Moreover, the catch records are supported by research data obtained from the Girnock Burn trap. Each year, the fish-trap intercepts a spawning population that is composed of spring salmon and a few grilse. Even today, spring salmon comprise the greater part of the spawners and grilse are no more frequent now than in the past. In short, if the habits of spring fish have altered to take other forms, they have not done so everywhere and the expected changes cannot be seen where they ought to be most easily recognised.

There is another possible way in which grilse or summer fish might supplant spring fish. The view of reciprocation between the spring and summer catches discussed above attributes the changes in run timing seen in some rivers to the flexibility of individual fish. It supposes that the very same fish that might otherwise have returned as spring fish have now become fish of other kinds. But the shifting balance theory proposed by Wright[14] offers a genetic perspective that is very different.

Wright's theory does not concern itself especially with salmon. But applied to salmon, it suggests that where spring catches have declined and summer catches have increased, the new summer fish may not be changed springers at all. Instead the new fish may be the progeny of other types of fish that always ran rivers during the summer. This view supposes that spring- and summer-running fish are distinguished genetically in some way. It also requires that the balance of advantage shifts from time to time among populations or among individuals of different genetic types when environmental conditions change.

Under these circumstances, some types of fish may be able to expand their range and their numbers at the expense of other types. At present, the spring fisheries may be changing to summer fisheries as a result of environmental changes that favour the summer-running habit or that are inimical to the lifestyle of spring fish. Presumably, at other times and under different circumstances, the direction of these changes can be reversed.

In those rivers with a traditionally uncomplicated fishery, the types of fish that find themselves favoured in the new situation – where they subsisted before – will not be strongly represented. As a result, the newly favoured types will not be well placed to take up the slack left by the types that were formerly dominant. A classic spring river, for example, may lack the genetic power-base required to generate new types of fish rapidly in large numbers. Fisheries on rivers like these will take longer to reach the appropriate new balance and they will be less productive during the transition.

The current plight of the spring fisheries is a matter of general concern. As a rule, the present situation is treated as one that has somehow gone wrong. And indeed, from a sporting point of view, this may be true – the value of traditional spring fisheries is being eroded. From a biological point of view, however, it is just as likely that problems are being put right. Perhaps the current changes are heartening evidence that salmon populations – like the blackcap populations described in Chapter 4 – retain a natural capacity for dealing with changing situations.

The changes taking place now are probably a replay of similar sorts of events that have taken place repeatedly over the centuries. We have seen how official catch records have been compiled for 40 years or so and how some single fisheries have been documented for a century or more. These may seem like long periods, but in biological terms, the information the catch records contain is a trivial fragment of the history of salmon populations – even the short history covering their occupancy of the rivers opened up in the wake of the last Ice Age. Measured against this scale of time, nothing that we know now can prepare us for what

Common seals on the foreshore of the Ythan estuary on Christmas Day. Contrary to popular belief, seals like these are not waiting to prey on passing salmon. Radio-tracking studies show that seals feed most often on long journeys out to sea lasting for several days. They eat a wide variety of marine species. Salmon forms part of their diet.

might happen in future. On a biological time-scale, we know almost nothing of how salmon live their lives. As a consequence, nothing that salmon populations may prove capable of doing ought to come as a surprise.

The manager's impotence in the face of these long time-scales does not relieve him of the responsibility for trying to help Nature along. Salmon populations can be managed appropriately on a realistic time-scale. Bearing in mind the wide range of performance that populations may be capable of developing, managers must work most of all to keep open the maximum number of biological options. In retrospect, the spring fishes' current difficulties may prove to be trivial. However, it is not possible to gauge whether current changes in the fisheries are temporary anomalies that will be restored in our lifetimes, or whether they are permanent – to the extent that permanence is a useful concept in this context.

Future changes may restore the fisheries to the previous status quo or they may lead populations and the fisheries they support in new, unexpected directions. In short, given the uncertainties, it would be a mistake to try to preserve particular fisheries in amber. No management measures are likely to thwart the forces of Nature. The wise manager, therefore, would do well to hedge his bets. His principal aim should be to conserve the genetic potential that populations represent. This guarantees populations the ability to continue their development with the same degree of latitude they have exercised in the past, and hopefully, with the same degree of success.

Populations can be supported directly through management work or by regulating the fisheries. In principle, a valid fishery crops stock to leave an adequate residue of spawners in every population. Even then there is a small biological price to pay for having a fishery at all. The spawning stock that remains after the fishery will always have a narrower genetic base than the pre-fishery stock. Unusual and infrequent genes will be inadvertently lost with the fish taken by anglers. This will be the case especially for small populations comprising few fish. On balance, of course, the price is worth paying. As a rule, the support anglers offer to salmon greatly outweighs any harm they may do.

As we have seen, river fisheries are mixed-stock fisheries that exploit individuals belonging to any of a number of separate reproductive units. When the abundance of a river's stock changes, it is very unlikely that all its populations will be affected to the same extent. In the way of these things, some populations will be affected to a greater extent than others. In particular, when abundance falls – even while stock levels still appear to remain generally adequate – some spawning populations may already be in trouble. It is the manager's duty to anticipate this and to act in good time.

Seals intersperse feeding expeditions with long periods of rest at favoured haul-out places where they will not be disturbed.

We have seen how salmon must pass a series of tests at all stages of their existence in order that their lives should reach a satisfactory conclusion. We have also seen how exploitation rates tend to rise when the number of returning salmon falls. It can be seen now that this situation is a paradox. When natural mortality increases, those few fish that prove best at surmounting all the obstacles are killed by anglers in greater proportions than usual – just short of their final goal. This seems a pity and it need not be the case.

In North America, in those places where salmon face special problems, the number and type of fish that each angler may retain is set by local statute. The purpose of these regulations is to secure the spawning stock and, with it, the future of the fishery. North American anglers have absorbed these regulations into their sport and their enjoyment of angling appears undiminished. Indeed, anglers everywhere appear to share the same spirit. Towards the end of the season, when coloured fish in failing condition are being captured, salmon are returned freely to the water wherever they are caught. From the salmon's point of view, it is not important when in the season it is spared but, in the context of population structure, timing matters very much. In Europe's spring-fishing rivers, most of those fish that are spared by the rods near the season's end are not of the same type as those that might be spared by the same rods near the season's start.

Anglers have it in their power to extend the restraint they show in autumn to other parts of the season. The catch-and-release philosophy of angling treats the salmon's capture and not its death as the climax of the sport. Catch-and-release is effective. Salmon can usually be returned to rivers without harm if they are fairly caught and carefully and properly handled. Anglers might offer practical, informal support to all spawning populations, and particularly to those that they know to be weak, by practising catch-and-release. Indeed, it may come to be viewed as a badge of distinction for anglers prepared, when necessary, to spare the lives of the fish that will become the founders of the next generation.

Catch-and-release will not be acceptable to all anglers, but it will have to be discussed. Indeed, it is only one of many issues that will have to be considered and resolved by anglers to enable fishery managers to lay their plans. The pressures on salmon have increased over the years. In particular, greater numbers of anglers have applied more intense efforts towards catching greater numbers of fish. It seems very likely that this trend will continue undiminished. Informed and effective management of salmon and salmon fisheries will be more important in future than ever before. As we have seen, most of the important biological issues are complex. Perhaps the framework we have explored in this book will be found useful in the coming debate.

Index